# THE KNIFE
# IN MY BACK

STACEY COVINGTON-LEE

Cover Design: The Final Wrap

Formatting/Typesetting: Under Cover Designs

ISBN – 978-1-7338811-0-4

Second Printing @ Copyright 2019

Published by SCL Novel Publications

Printed in the United States of America

Stacey Covington-Lee
n o v e l s

*To those that have gone before me,*
*but continue to inspire me.*

*Timothy Covington Sr.*
*Lizzie McCoy*
*Claudis McCoy*
*T'Irma Covington*
*Claudius Covington*

# PROLOGUE

"Oh my God, answer the phone...please answer the phone."

"Hello"

"Brook, he's dead! I killed him. Tell me what to do?"

"Slow down Tameka, who's dead? What are you talking about?'

"Titus, the guy I met tonight. We came back to his place to have a couple of beers and he started doing some freaky shit! I was so scared; I just wanted to get him off of me. I didn't mean to kill him. HELP ME!"

"Okay, I'm calling the police."

"Hell no, I can't go to jail...I gotta get out of here! I know we've had our problems, but now is not the time to turn on me. I shouldn't have even called you."

"Just calm down. Give me the address; I'm coming to get you."

After hanging up the phone, Brook called Rodney. He was a good friend that wanted to be more, but Brook couldn't make herself go there with him. Friends were all they would ever be. Rodney came right over in the campus security car and Brook knew then that he couldn't drive it to pick up her friend. She explained the situation knowing that she could trust Rodney with her life and then she gave him the keys to her Benz. Within the hour, Rodney returned with a shaken Tameka. He gave Brook her keys, reassuring her that no one saw him and he then handed Brook a paper bag. He gently whispered "This is for you and your protection should anything ever come up". Rodney kissed Brook on the cheek, turned and walked away.

# CHAPTER ONE

Graduation day! This was indeed the biggest day in the girl's lives. They had worked so hard to get to this point, or at least one of them had. Brook was steadfast in her studying and work ethic, while Tameka got here by hook or crook. But now all that mattered was that they were here. And who would have ever guessed it with the way that they started out.

Four years ago, Brook arrived on the Spelman campus with her parents in tow. She had tried her best to convince them that she could make the drive alone and get her room situated without their help. But she knew all along that they would never go for that, she was, after all, their only baby. They had planned and prayed for her since their wedding night and when she finally made her entrance into the world three years later, they were overjoyed. They provided her with everything a child could ever need or want. Brook wore the finest clothes, lived in the most upscale neighborhood Baltimore had to offer. She had attended the most prominent Christian schools, but that was just the material. The best thing about Brook's parents was that they taught her about love, respect, family and loyalty. This child knew above all else in the world that she was loved. And the way her parents loved one another taught her what marriage was

supposed to be. She would never come right out and tell them, but she was glad that
Mommy and Daddy were here to see her get started with the next phase of her life.

After retrieving the keys to her dorm room, Brook and her parents began to unload her belongings and set up the side of the room she had chosen. After all, the first one there gets to pick the side they want…right? They had arranged her stereo, television, refrigerator and other belongings just as she'd wanted them. Katherine, Brook's mom, had even purchased matching bed sets so the room would be well coordinated. A little presumptuous she thought but what the heck, she wanted it to look nice. Just as they were putting the finishing touches on the room,

Brook's roommate appeared in the door.

"Well, I guess you decided this gone be your side, no scissor, paper, rock or nothing huh?"

"I'm sorry, did I miss something? Do I know you?"

"Don't be sorry, I'm your roommate, Tameka and I just meant that you didn't give me no say in what side of the room would be mine. Looks like you just took over."

"Well Tameka, I'm Brook and these are my parents Mr. and Mrs. Mansfield. I didn't mean to take over, but you know how it is, the early bird gets the worm."

"Yeah, I guess. Snooze you lose. Well, it's nice to meet ya'll anyway."

Needless to say, Katherine's next thought was that she wished they had private rooms available. Why Brook wanted a room-mate in the first place, she didn't quite understand. You can still make friends and bond with others in a private room. Not that Katherine was a snob, far from it, but this girl just seemed real rough around the edges and she didn't want Brook to have any unnecessary conflicts.

As Tameka dragged her two duffle bags and backpack into the room, it was clear to everyone that she had not had the advantages that Brook had. She was dressed well enough in her jeans, halter top and K-Swiss sneakers but her luggage wasn't exactly a matching Gucci set.

Tameka was about five foot seven inches tall and a perfect size six. Brook couldn't help but admire her well-proportioned body. Brook also took notice of the smooth Hershey chocolate complexion that covered Tameka and her almond shaped eyes and high cheekbones. Although Tameka seemed to be a little tough and rough she was a lovely girl that could probably make a fortune as a model.

"Do you need any help with your things young lady?" asked Martin, Brook's father.

"No, thank you, I've got it."

Tameka thought it was nice of Mr. Mansfield to offer but she didn't want anybody thinking that she needed help with anything right now, especially someone she perceived as "snooty". As Tameka began to unpack her things, she would sneak glances over at the perfect little family, but she mostly concentrated on Brook. She first noticed the long, dark hair flowing down Brooks back. She estimated Brook to be about five foot five inches tall and a slim but well put together size five. Brook had very soft, feminine features, gentle eyes and a flawless honey complexion. She was beautiful and classy, a combination that could easily make a girl jealous.

As the Mansfield's prepared to leave, they reassured their daughter that they were only a phone call away. They made sure that she had her emergency credit card, spending money and a blank check from dad's business account to cover her books. After several hugs, kisses and a few tears, they were off. But before leaving they each gave Tameka a soft, kind hug and permission to call them if the need ever arose. This behavior from strangers was new to Tameka, but she found it to be quite comforting.

Once alone in their room, the girls started talking and attempting to learn a little about one another. Surprisingly, the conversation flowed easily. Brook learned that Tameka was there on a full scholarship and had a work-study job to help earn spending money. Although she arrived alone, Tameka stressed that she was not alone in this world. Her mother would be by later after work. Tameka was one of four kids, same mom, but all different dads. Her mother was by no means a whore or a loose woman, just a hard working woman that made a couple of bad decisions in her quest for love. She raised her kids alone in a housing complex in the heart of Atlanta. So far, Tameka was the one that her mother was hanging all her hopes on. She was the first to graduate high school and was now attending college. Tameka's three older brothers decided to live by the streets. One is now serving time for armed robbery, one is a known drug dealer and the youngest boy died two years ago when the cops busted a street fight and one of their stray bullets hit him. Needless to say, Brook found all of this nothing less than amazing.

She was hearing things that she'd only read about or seen on the 6:00 news. She couldn't help but admire Tameka for making it this far.

As months and years passed, Brook learned things about Tameka that she didn't admire....most things she learned, she despised. After coming up with ground rules that they both agreed to, Brook often called Tameka to the carpet for breaking one rule or another. Tameka was constantly in Brook's clothes, a huge no, no, interrupting Brook's private moments and hitting her up for cash as if she were the local ATM. And for the life of her, Brook could not understand why someone as smart as Tameka was constantly cheating on tests and trying to buy mid-term reports instead of just studying and doing work that mostly came easy to her. Brook threatened many times to move to a different room, but they had actually bonded on a real friend-ship level and Brook couldn't bring herself to actually move out. Just when she was convinced that Tameka was just using her in one way or another, Tameka would do something like bring

Brook a beautiful ballerina figurine to add to her beloved collection. It was a friendship she just hadn't been able to let go of.

But now, here they were, graduation day. Ms. Williams, Tameka's mom, was so proud. She was running around helping the girls get ready. She had always treated Brook as if she were her daughter too. Ms. Williams was more than happy to fill in until Brook's parents arrived. Brook was a little surprised and started to feel disappointed. She had spoken with her parents no more than three hours ago and they assured her that they would be there on time. Nothing would stop them from seeing their baby girl walk across that stage and receive that hard earned degree. The door swung open and pulled Brook out of her thoughts. There stood Mia, another of Brooks good friends dressed out in her cap and gown. She was all smiles and advised the girls that it was time go. Brook walked over and gave her a big hug and Tameka gave her an ugly eye roll. Mia was not one of Tameka's favorite people, probably because she seemed to be on to every scheme

Tameka tried to pull and often warned Brook about her so called friend. But this was graduation day and Tameka shook off the bad vibes, ready now to be nice to everyone, even Mia.

After the ceremony everyone began to disperse and the graduates sought out their families in the crowd. Brook still hadn't seen her parents and just as she started to walk toward another crowd of people, her path was blocked by two uniformed police officers.

"Ma'am, are you Brook Mansfield?"

"Yes, is there something I can help you with?"

Brook's mind immediately went to the night of Tameka's accidental murder. She couldn't believe that after all this time this was coming to haunt her on the happiest day of her life.

"Miss Mansfield, is there somewhere we can talk?"

"Yes, let's step over here where there's less traffic. Now, how can I help you?"

"We hate to inform you that there's been an accident.

Approximately two hours ago your parent's car was hit by a truck that lost control on the highway. They were taken to Grady Hospital's trauma unit…"

"So they are still alive?"

"Ma'am, I'm sorry. The doctors did all that they could. Their injuries were just too severe. I'm so sorry."

# CHAPTER TWO

It had been three months since the death of Brook's parents. In an effort to start living life on her own, Brook decided to stay in Atlanta permanently. She'd gone back to Maryland to arrange her parent's funeral and tie up all of the business' loose ends. While there, she met with her parent's lawyer and learned that everything had been left entirely to her. The business, which she learned was worth an estimated ten million dollars, the house and $2.3 million in cash, stocks and bonds. She wasn't prepared for this kind of wealth and could find no joy in it since she got it only through the death of her heroes.

The home would remain there with the personal belongings packed away and all of the furnishings covered, but left in place. Brook had to admit to herself that she knew nothing about running her father's construction company and she didn't want to run his life's work in the ground. With that in mind, she met with Benjamin Ross, her father's partner and her pretend uncle, and they worked out a buy out that both she and her attorney thought was an excellent deal. Now the business was all Uncle Benjamin's and she didn't have the fear of messing up what her father had built.

With all of the business handled, Brook chose a few personal items of her parents that meant a lot to them and now to her and packed them with her other things. She took a cab to the cemetery, stopping first by a florist to purchase some of their favorite flowers. Once Brook arrived, she broke down crying like never before. She laid her body across her parent's grave as if to hug them for the last time. It was so hard for her to pull herself up. All she really wanted was for the ground to open up and suck her in. The realization of going on without her mommy and daddy was almost more than Brook could bear. She finally pulled herself up, but as she walked away she knew that she was leaving her heart behind.

Mia was kind enough to pick Brook up from the airport and allow her to stay in the extra bedroom of her town home until Brook could decide on a new home of her own.

"How was your flight, sweetie?"

"It was good, you know how it goes. Go through a million security checks and then just wait until take off."

"I know it had to be difficult for you, but did you get all of your business taken care of, or will you have to return to tie things up?"

"I got everything settled, but Mia, it was the hardest thing I've ever had to do. Packing up my parents things, selling my father's business, just knowing that they were gone…forever. It still seems so unreal, still beyond my comprehension."

"I'm so sorry I wasn't able to be up there with you, but I'm here now for whatever you need. Was Tameka of any help or comfort to you when she went up for those two weeks?"

"You know, she tried her best. I was glad to have a friend there, but the warm and fuzzy compassionate thing just isn't really her style."

As they drove through the streets of Southwest Atlanta, Brook found herself admiring all of the beautiful new neighbor-hoods recently constructed. The buildup of this area was amazing. When Mia turned into her own subdivision of town homes, Brook gave her a *you go girl* look, proud of her for choosing such a great area and being able to do it all on her own. The streets were lined with dogwood trees and paved sidewalks. Each home was of all brick construction with two car garages, they were lovely.

"Well, here we are, let's get your things and get you all settled in. I tried to fix the room up for you as nice as I could. I just really want you to be comfortable and feel at home."

The girls got all of Brook's things out of the car and into her new, temporary bedroom. They then decided to sit and relax for a while with some hot tea and Brook's favorite Chips Ahoy cookies. Mia thought cookies and tea to be a strange combination, but hey, whatever made Brook happy. Mia was just glad for the tea; it's what gave her comfort on overcast, rainy days. One of the reasons Mia settled in Atlanta was for the hot, sunny summer days and fairly mild winters. Unfortunately, this summer had been filled with an unusually high number of rainy days which meant that she had been drinking tea more than ever before.

Mia and Brook had met at Spelman freshman year. It was during orientation that they were divided into groups with Brook, Mia and Tameka being in the same group with about four other girls. Brook just seemed to be drawn to Mia. Mia was a tall, statuesque girl. She was an even six feet tall with beautiful hazel eyes and a caramel complexion that was as smooth as Chinese silk. Just the way she talked had the ability to suck you right into her world. Needless to say, she was very popular with the guys, but very selective when it came to dating. That is one thing that she and Brook had in common and something that Tameka just didn't understand.

Tameka didn't feel about Mia as Brook did, she viewed her as competition. Competition for not only the interest of men, but the friendship of Brook. She didn't feel that there was room enough for the both of them in Brook's life. One had to be more important than the other and Tameka just couldn't come in second to Mia. Brook had too much to offer and Tameka wanted it all for herself. Mia picked up on these competitive vibes a long time ago. She felt that Tameka wasn't the friend she pretended to be, but far be it for her to try and come between Brook and any of her other friends. Besides, whenever she tried to gently mention to Brook to look out for Tameka, she was quickly told that Tameka was the best friend that she knew how to be and that everyone just needed to give her a chance.

"So, does Tameka know that you're back in town yet?"

"No, I told her I'd call her when I got back. I'll give her a call later; I want to relax for a while. You know, sit and talk with you, play catch up."

"Child, there's nothing to catch up on, I'm just an old lady with no life outside of work."

"Well, girl, I'm going to let you be old by yourself. We aren't but twenty-three and I'm just getting ready to start living. But I never thought I'd have to start without any family to fall back on. I tell you, there's something to be said for brothers and sisters because I sure wish I had one or two right now."

"I can only imagine how hard this all has to be for you. I know I'm not family and we're not blood, but since I have no siblings either, why don't we work on building our own sisterhood. You know I love you and that I'm here for you."

"I know, I love you too and I would love to be your sister. That's something that we can definitely work on, but right now we are going to change the subject because I don't want to cry. I'm all cried out. I just want to keep it light and enjoy this little time of relaxation. Is that cool with you?"

"Oh yeah, I can get with that, light and relaxing. Sounds like a damn good plan."

They laughed and talked on for a while until Brook's body let her know that she was in need of a good night's sleep. She gave Mia a tight hug and said thanks yet again for letting her stay there a while. Brook then cleaned up her dishes and headed up to bed wondering what tomorrow, next week, next month would bring.

# CHAPTER THREE

Tameka woke up, rubbed her eyes and looked around her room in disgust. No one could have ever told her that she'd end up back in Grady Homes housing project. She was most confident that once she graduated and moved out of the dorm, she would go straight into some fabulous condo or town home. But here she was back with her mother and hating every second of it. She could not stand looking around at the dingy beige walls and torn mini blinds. For goodness sake, she'd had the same furniture since she was eight, didn't she deserve something better?

She turned the bed side radio to her favorite morning show. She just loved the crew at HOT 107.5. They always helped her shake those early morning blues. After opening what was left of the blinds, she looked out to try and gauge the weather conditions for the day. Tameka danced her way into the bathroom and turned on the shower. After completing her grooming routine, she went to her small closet and chose a nice fuchsia pant suit and black pumps for work. Once she'd completed her makeup, Tameka took a long look at herself in a full length mirror and decided that she was fabulous.

"Good morning, baby, how did you sleep?"

"I slept alright, Mama, how about you; did you get a good night's rest?"

"Oh I guess, after I finally found a good sleeping position and slept for about an hour, I was woke by a real bad cramp in my leg. Child, you know how those thangs do me, I've had problems with them for a while now..."

As her mom went on talking about her night, all Tameka could think about was how she wished she'd never asked her the question in the first place. It was a simple question that required only a simple answer. She was not in the mood for all of this senseless chatter. There was too much on her mind and too many plans that had to be made.

"Are you listening to me, girl? If you ask somebody something at least be polite enough to listen to their answer."

"Damn, Mama, I just wanted a yes or a no, I didn't need a dictation on every second of your night."

"Oh, now wait a minute, I know you not gone stand in my house and curse me, have you lost your mind. I'm your mama and you will respect me!"

"Okay, okay, you're right and I'm sorry. I didn't mean to curse you, it just slipped out, it won't happen again."

Tameka grabbed a chipped plate out of the drain basket and started to fix herself a plate of the breakfast her mom had prepared. She loved the way that her mom still cared enough to get up early and prepare her favorite foods. Mom always said that breakfast was the best meal of the day. Of course, she was one of the few old school folks that still fried chicken to eat that early. Tameka grabbed a glass of orange juice and took a seat at the small table.

"I saw that housing magazine on the counter, are you trying to find a place of your own?"

"I guess I'm going to have to start seriously looking. God knows I can't stay here much longer. No offense. I just wish Brook would get her act together and move out of Mia's already. She agreed that we could be roommates and that's what I was trying to hold out for. It would mean a lot less money coming out of my pocket."

"Child, you can easily afford to move into your own place and not just rent some apartment. You can buy yourself a nice new home all your own."

"Yeah, Mama, I could, but why spend that kind of money when Brook can spend hers. That girls worth millions now and she'll let me live with her in her nice new home for next to nothing. I'm trying to get her to buy this in town loft; the thing is huge with all of the amenities you could ever want. Check it out, the building even has a doorman and security entrance, it's very exclusive."

As Tameka rose from the table to clear her plate, she saw her mom looking at her out the corner of her eye. She didn't like the look of disgust that was being thrown her way.

"Now what's wrong with you?"

"Just listen to yourself. Don't you have any compassion for what that girls going through? She just lost her family, her mama and daddy and all you can think about is how to spend her money. You better be careful, girl, you know what the good book say's, the love of money is the root of all evil and right now you're loving her money just a little too much."

"Yes, I have compassion, if I didn't I wouldn't have gone all the way to Baltimore to be with her in the first place. I've tried my best to be a good friend to her and to help her through her grieving period, but it's been ten months now, how much time does she need!"

Tameka grabbed her briefcase and headed for the door, she didn't want to hear one more word from her mother. She picked up her car keys and looked over her shoulder toward her mom, "Why can't you try to see things from my point of view just once?" She walked out slamming the door behind her.

As Tameka pulled into the parking deck, she tried to brush off the bad vibes for the second time today. That's a damn shame, it's only 8:50am and she's already had a bad day. But she knew she had to get it together quickly, she didn't want her managers or co-workers asking if she was okay or trying to pry into her private life. That's not how you get ahead in business, her motto…always be professional.

Making her way through the CNN building, Tameka stopped long enough to grab a cup of coffee. As she glided on to her office around the corner from the news studio, she couldn't help but smile. This job was the one really good thing in her life right now. She'd always wanted to work in television and now she was actually doing it. Who would have believed that she'd be a news producer for such a huge organization? Producer today, head anchor tomorrow. The current noon day anchor had better watch her back because Tameka would have her job one way or another and then on to the top spot. The girl had ambitions and wouldn't stop until they were reached. As she closed the door behind her, the phone rang, she picked up and was actually glad to hear Brook's voice.

"Good morning, girl, have you settled into work yet?"

"Oh, just getting started. What's up with you?"

"I have a late day interview and wanted to see if you'd meet me and Mia for dinner? Say 6:30 at Dailey's? We can have a great meal and discuss my living arrangements, what do you say?"

"Count me in, I'll meet you guys at the bar area. Later, chick."

# CHAPTER FOUR

Brook wrapped herself in a thick, soft bath robe and headed down stairs to grab a cup of coffee and a bagel. As she sat down at the kitchen table she found herself once again looking around and admiring Mia's decorating skills. The maple cabinets, granite counter tops and black appliances were all accented by the black and gold window treatments. Mia had even re-covered the seat cushions of her kitchen chairs in a rich, deep gold fabric that looked fabulous with her glass and gold leaf table. Brook shook her head knowing that she could never decorate her place and make it look like anything nice. That was her mother's cup of tea. That woman could make any room look like it belonged in a home fashion magazine. God, how she missed her parents, but she wasn't going to dwell on that now. Instead of allowing herself to think about her parents, she picked up the yellow pages and turned to the home interiors section. She proceeded to write down the names of several interior design groups that could potentially help her decorate the new home that she had yet to buy.

While Brook nibbled at her food, she reviewed the interview questions that Mia had written down for her. She wanted to be totally prepared for her interview this afternoon. Brook had only gone on one other interview since her return, but it was only for practice. It was for an accounting position in a small doctor's office. Definitely not a job she had wanted, but again, it was a good way to sharpen those interview skills. Today's interview, now that's a different story. This was for a Senior Staff Accountant position with a major law firm and the person to snatch this position would receive a major salary boost once they earned their CPA. Not that Brook needed a large salary, but she had to admit to herself that she would enjoy the prestige. She had heard about the position from Mia who had convinced her to go for it. This was Mia's employer and she loved her work and the people she worked with. Mia went on to study for and pass the CPA exam as soon as they'd graduated. She was extended many job offers, but was glad everyday that she went with the law firm. Mia was very well respected there, so when a position was left open by another employee's sudden exit, Mia immediately thought of Brook. She told her manager of her intelligent, capable friend who was currently preparing to take the CPA exam. The manager had Brook to fax a resume and immediately scheduled an interview. Brook was a little hesitant about the whole thing at first, but Mia helped her realize that she needed to really be among the living and she couldn't do that in a bath robe looking at soap operas all day. This was a next step that Brook was becoming more and more excited about by the minute.

Brook arrived fifteen minutes early for her interview so that she would have time to settle herself and get her nerves in check. As she was escorted to the interviewer's office, she spotted Mia who gave her an encouraging thumbs up. Approximately thirty-five minutes later the office door opened. Brook shook hands with the manager, said thank you and turned to leave. Mia stopped her right before she left the building to ask how things went.

"Well, how did it go? Did you like Susie? When did she tell you she'd make decision?"

"Good grief, girl, slow down, take a breath. I'm going to run over to the mall for a while, give you time to end your work day and then we can head over to the restaurant. I'll tell you everything once we sit down in front of a couple of Amaretto Sours."

"Is Tameka going to meet us there?"

"Yes and I want you two to play nice, you hear me!"

"I'm always nice; it's Ms. Tameka you better worry about. Hell, I'm an angel; you don't have to be warning me to be nice."

"Oh be quiet, child, must you go on and on. I'll pick you up in an hour, okay?"

"Yes ma'am, I'll see you then. Oh, and try not to buy out the mall, save something for the rest of us."

"Ha-ha, you're just a regular comedian. Bye."

Brook strolled through the mall admiring all of the beautiful window displays but not really interested in buying anything for herself. She had a specific purchase in mind and wasn't going to allow herself to be distracted. As she casually scanned the items in a keepsake shop, she spotted a small, crystal bell with gold trim. It was so delicate, so feminine. Was it really possible for something like a bell to remind her of her mother? Brook just had to smile, she guessed it was possible. After all, her mom was the most delicate person she'd ever known. She replaced the bell and moved on through the store until she came across what she'd originally come for. She picked up the Armani statue of a gorgeous black woman named Lacey. Mia had been admiring this statue for months but just couldn't make herself drop the $1,500.00 it cost to buy it. What better way to say thanks for her hospitality and setting up the interview than this. Brook thought it was perfect and knew that it would be appreciated. She made her purchase and left to go pick up her friend.

Brook was many things but patient wasn't one of them. She'd been sitting in her car listening to the radio for at least fifteen minutes. She was just about to call Mia's office when she spotted her walking out of the glass double doors. Brook started the car, unlocked the door and motioned for Mia to hurry up.

"Girl, stop waving your hands at me."

"Well, bring your butt on, do you know how long I've been sitting here? You were supposed to be out here twenty minutes ago."

"Ten minutes ago and it's not like I was just hanging out, I was working. You've got to learn a little patience; everyone isn't working on Brook's time clock you know. So get over it and let's go."

Brook pulled into the parking deck down the block from Daily's, relieved that they'd finally made it through the rush hour traffic. Before they got out of the car Brook reached back and gently handed Mia a bag. Before Mia could say a word Tameka knocked on the car window.

"Hey ladies, what's up? What's in the bag, Mia?"

"I don't know yet, Brook just handed it to me."

Mia opened the bag and pulled out the fragile statue. A smile spread across her face as she looked at Brook in amazement. Tameka also gave Brook a look but it was not one of amazement but one of disgust.

"So Brook, what's the occasion, why such an extravagant gift?"

Brook hated having to share this moment with Tameka, she knew that Tameka's greatest concern would be why she didn't get a gift as well.

"It's just my way of saying thank you to you Mia for opening your home to me and getting me the interview with Susie. I really appreciate how you've put yourself out there for me. Thank you!"

"Girl, you know that my home is your home and I'll always do anything I can for you. You're my sister girl."

"Oh hell can ya'll hurry and finish this Kodak moment. I'm hungry and could use a good stiff drink."

"I swear, Tameka, you could ruin a wet dream. Why do you always have to be so cold?"

"Well I don't know, Mia, maybe it's just my nature like being a kiss ass is yours."

"I should have expected that from you, once a hood rat always a hood rat"

"Shut up! Both of you just shut up, can't we just have a nice night out without all of the drama. You two have been doing this since freshman year and I'm sick of it. Now either act like you have some sense or I'm leaving. I'm not listening to this crap all night."

Tameka took a deep breath in an attempt to calm herself down. The last thing she wanted was for Brook to leave. She needed to hear what Brook's future living arrangements would be. She had to make sure that she would be part of those plans.

"Look, I'm sorry. I shouldn't have gone off like that. I've just had a long hard day but I shouldn't have taken it out on you two. Can we just go have a drink and grab some dinner?"

They were seated at nice little corner table where they ordered a round of drinks and munched on bread sticks in silence for the first ten minutes. Finally, Brook broke the cloud of silence hanging over their table by telling Mia that the time had come for her to find her own home. She told her friends that she'd hired a realtor and was looking at town homes and condos in some of the finer Atlanta suburbs. Tameka, however, preferred living in the city and finally convinced Brook to look at a couple of the new in town lofts. She considered this a small victory; she knew once she got Brook away from Mia, she'd be able to use those powers of persuasion more effectively and ultimately end up sharing a dream home with Brook. Rent free of course.

As the girls finally started to loosen up and enjoy some easy flowing conversation they were interrupted by an amazing looking gentleman.

"Hello ladies. Please forgive me for interrupting your dinner, but I felt compelled to come

over and introduce myself. My name is Eric Banks and I would be honored if you all allowed me
to buy you another round of drinks."

Tameka blurted out just as loud and ghetto as she could "you can buy the drinks if you come sit next to me."

"I'd be delighted."

Eric pulled up a chair and opted to sit more in the middle of the women than up under Tameka. The ladies couldn't help but admire what a fine looking guy he was. Eric stood 6 feet 2 inches tall with short curly hair and a soft mocha complexion. The man could easily star in any toothpaste commercial with that perfect smile he flashed. Mr. Banks was definitely the finest thing they'd seen in a long time, it was easy to tell that under that thousand dollar suit was a body God gave only to super heroes.

"Now that you know who I am, may I ask your names?"

They introduced themselves one by one, but it was Brook's hand he seemed to hold onto just a little longer than necessary.

"So Eric, what do you do for a living?" Tameka asked bluntly.

"I'm a financial advisor."

"Does that pay well, very well, or just okay?"

Brook and Mia looked at each other in disbelief and then at Tameka as if to tell her to shut up. Eric, who was becoming annoyed with Tameka's line of questioning, answered her in a short, sharp tone "I do alright for myself." He then stood to his feet and turned to Brook.

"I didn't mean to be this big of an interruption to your evening, I just wanted to introduce myself and ask if it would be possible for us to speak again?"

"Eric, I do appreciate the drinks, but I'm not in the habit of giving out my number."

"I understand, how about I give you my card and if you decide you want to talk, just call me, I'll always be available for you." he said with a wink and then turned and walked away.

"You a damn trip Brook, why you didn't give the brother no play?"

"That's not why I'm out tonight Tameka, I just wanted to spend a little time with my friends and have a nice meal. Now that I've done that I'm ready to go home."

"Well, before you go, can you at least tell me when our first meeting with the realtor is, I'm ready to start house hunting."

"I'll call you and let you know. Now come on guys, I'm tired."

"Ya'll go on, I'm gonna hang out at the bar a while."

"Suit yourself," chimed Mia "we're gone, good night."

# CHAPTER FIVE

"Tameka, Brook called last night to tell you something about a meeting with an agent, what's that about?"

"Nothing much, I'm just gonna go look at some houses with her. You know, help her decide where to move."

"So does that mean that you decided to find your own house?"

"No! It means that I'm gonna help her find our house. She's more than willing to have me as a roommate, so I don't know why you have such a problem with it, Mama."

"I wouldn't have a problem with it if I knew that you weren't just trying to use her. She's been too good a friend to you and been through too much to have you use her like some old dish rag."

"Gee, Mom, I just love how you think so highly of me, it makes me warm and tingly all over. By the way, if you think so little of me, what does that say about you and your parenting skills?"

"Alright Tameka, I think you were on your way out the door, I think you need to keep heading out before you find yourself spitting up teeth. I'm sick of your mouth; I've worked too hard to bring you up right to have you disrespecting me at every turn.

I don't care who you move with, just move outta here as soon as you can"

"Mama, I'm sorry, I…"

"Leave!"

Tameka grabbed her purse, hung her head in shame and walked out of the door. She could not believe that her mother had just told her to get out, could not believe that she had been so disrespectful to the woman that had sacrificed so much for her. This was definitely a low point for Tameka and even she realized that. As she slid into her car and closed the door she couldn't help but shed a tear or two. Tameka hated crying but she hated hurting her mom even more. She flipped open her cell phone and dialed information.

"May I have the number for A Daisy A Day florist?"

Tameka knew that this wouldn't completely make up for her behavior, but two dozen long stem yellow roses was a start. She pulled off and headed down to the office to tie up some loose ends and she would then be off the rest of the day. Tameka wanted to make sure that she and Brook would have plenty of time for their house hunting expedition.

As soon as Tameka walked into her office, Craig stepped in and closed the door. Craig was a co-worker and a frequent lover when Tameka didn't have someone better on the hook. Although she didn't really have eyes for another man right now, she hadn't had a rendezvous with Craig in a while.

"Why do I get the feeling that you're avoiding me, Tameka? A couple of months ago you couldn't get enough of me and now you won't even return my calls, what's up with that?"

"Craig I've been busy. I haven't had time to help you get your rocks off."

"Oh, so it's like that, you think I'm just trying to get my rocks off?"

"Look honey, that's just the nature of our relationship. We help each other get off. You've known all along that it's never been anything serious. Don't start trippin' now."

"You can't tell me that as much as we've been together you've never developed any real feelings about me, about us. I refuse to believe you're that cold."

"Craig, believe what you want. I don't have time for this, I've got to finish this report real quick and get out of here. And if you really are developing so called real feelings for me, then stop. I don't want a relationship with you. We had a lot of fun together so just hang on to the memories and let's move on with our separate lives."

"You are one cold bitch!"

"I've been called worse; please close the door behind you."

Craig turned to leave but suddenly changed the direction of his steps. He instead closed the blinds to Tameka's office and hastily locked the door. Before Tameka could even question what he was doing, he leaped across her desk and pushed her up against the wall with his hands around her neck. Barely able to breath, Tameka started trying to fight him off. When she did manage to scratch him, he smacked her across the face and tightened the grip around her neck. He then took his right hand and forced her skirt up and his hand in her panties. As he angrily forced his hand in her he began to tell her what a whore she really was and warned her to watch her back. He then threw her to the floor and cleaned his hand on her blouse.

"Bitch, if you open your mouth to anyone about us or what just happened between us I'll kill you. I advise you to learn how to treat people before you really get hurt…you silly whore."

Craig turned and headed out of the door leaving Tameka to scramble to her feet and get herself together before anyone saw her. She headed out to the ladies room where she splashed her face with water to wash away her tears. She had never been so angry with herself. How could she allow that punk ass boy to hurt her like that? He may have thought he'd gotten the better of her but she knew she'd have the last laugh. He didn't realize who he was screwing with but before it was all over, Tameka would make him regret the day he laid eyes on her.

## CHAPTER SIX

Brook followed behind her realtor stopping here and there to look at different features and amenities that the house had to offer. It was the first house she would be looking at today and didn't want to get too excited about it. But she had to admit that it was a lovely little house that gave her a warm and secure feeling. The neighborhood was so beautiful but Brook wasn't sure that she wanted to live all the way up in Alpharetta. Once she started working, she'd have one hell of a commute and she wasn't at all patient when it came to rush hour traffic.

As Brook and her agent headed out of the house, Tameka came running in. She was rushing so that she almost knocked the agent down.

"Oops, I'm sorry, did I hurt you?"

"No, I'm alright."

Brook helped her agent pick up her things and took that time to introduce the two ladies.

"Tameka this is Lauren Rush, realtor extraordinaire. Lauren this is Tameka, my college roommate and friend."

The ladies shook hands and exchanged pleasantries. Tameka then took a quick look around the house and re-joined Brook and Lauren at the door.

"So, Brook, how do you feel about this one?"

"I like it, I think it's a really nice house but before you came in, I was telling Lauren that I wasn't sure I wanted to live this far from town."

"Thank God for that. I sure wouldn't want to live way out in these boonies."

"Excuse me, I don't mean to jump in here but are you guys going to share whatever home you buy."

"Well, it's a strong possibility. It depends on where I decide to buy and if it's a set up that will allow us both a decent amount of privacy."

"So, do I need to re-write the paper work to include Tameka as a buyer?"

Tameka suddenly jumps in and screams "No". Lauren was taken aback by her sudden outburst. She couldn't understand why she wouldn't want part in her own home.

"May I ask why? If your name were on it then that extra income would mean more house for the two of you and it would also help you with your taxes. There are countless benefits."

"Well, I'm not interested in all of that. This is a deal that me and Brook came up with. She wants to own a home and I want to temporarily share it. There is no need for you to be concerned about anything else."

A look of shock crept across both Brook and Lauren's faces. Lauren was only trying to point out things that could help them both. Tameka's poor attitude was totally uncalled for.

"Tameka, you don't have to speak to her like that. It is unnecessary and downright rude."

"It's okay Brook, I like to know the type of folks I'm dealing with and I know now. Sorry if I offended you Miss. Tameka, just trying to do my job."

"Apology accepted. Where do we go from here? Hopefully somewhere closer to the city."

Brook was so disgusted with Tameka; she looked at her and replied dryly "Yeah, you can follow us."

The ladies got into their cars and headed down GA 400 back to town. Brook and Lauren rode in silence. Brook welcomed this moment and used the quiet time to get her head together and was sure that Lauren wanted the same. She angered herself by allowing Tameka to get under her skin so often and easily. It was times like these that made her question whether they would be able to live together in peace. Brook refused to give up her peace and solitude just to live with Tameka's drama and attitude. But enough about Tameka, she wanted to soak up this beautiful day and enjoy the ride. The sun was shining bright, the air was crisp and Brook had plenty to be excited about. It's not every day that you get to decide on your first new home.

"Ms. Brook, you're looking pretty happy over there, managed to change that mood huh?"

"Yeah, I don't like to stay angry or upset. Besides, I actually have a lot to be happy about."

"Yes, you do and I want you to stay happy, but I really need to talk to you about that Ms. Tameka."

"I know, you don't think that I should let her live with me unless her name is on the house. She needs to be responsible for the property as well. Trust me, I've heard it already."

"Now see, I wasn't going to say any of that, in fact, just the opposite. The best thing that you can do is to have your home in your name alone. It's not like you need her income, but please make sure that you have a lease drawn up. This lease needs to be very specific with regard to the amount of rent you'll charge, the length of time she can stay and most importantly, the terms under which you can throw her ass out as soon as she misses a month's rent."

Brook burst out laughing; no one had quite broken it down like Lauren just did. She was laughing so hard that tears came to her eyes. All Brook could imagine was the shocked look on Tameka's face when she told her she'd have to pay rent. Everyone had told her that Tameka was going to try and get a free ride and now she believed it herself. But for someone who'd known

Tameka all of thirty minutes to determine that she wanted to live for free was just hilarious to Brook.

"Okay Brook, I'm glad I could make you laugh, but I'm serious as a heart attack. As your realtor and friend it's my job to look out for your best interest and I don't think that Ms. Tameka is in your best interest. Far be it for me to put down your girlfriend, but I have to say what I feel."

"Well preach it then girl," Brook said with laughter in her voice.

"I'm serious Brook."

"I know and if it will make you feel better I already have an attorney working on the papers. I love Tameka but I won't be used by anyone."

The ladies looked at three more houses and two in town loft condos. Brook loved them all, but still felt she needed to see a couple more, so they made an appointment for Saturday morning. Tameka saw exactly where she wanted to live and was annoyed by the delay in Brook's decision making. But what else was new, Tameka was always annoyed when she didn't immediately get her way.

# CHAPTER SEVEN

"I'm so very proud of you and happy for you. Here's to you, my friend, my confidant, my sister in God and now my co-worker."

Mia and Brook clinked their glasses together and each took long sips of cool water. After Brook received the phone call offering her the position at Mia's firm, Mia insisted on taking her out to dinner to celebrate. They had met back at the house to shower and change for a nice evening out. Brook had never been to Harriston's and Mia thought it would be a nice, lively place to dine. Brook had been dressing so drab lately, not like the fashion plate she was known to be. Mia was very pleased to see her in a pair of low rise, boot cut jeans with a beautiful off the shoulder, pink cashmere sweater and three inch heel ankle boots. Mia wasn't looking bad herself in black stretch cargo pants with a beautiful white wrap shirt that tied on the side. She had even

treated herself to an exquisite pair of Gucci pumps. Needless to say, these women were phenomenal.

"So, what finally made you break down and buy those pumps girl? Lord knows you've been eyeing them for the longest."

"Well, if you must know girlfriend, I'll be getting a big fat referral check once you sign your acceptance letter from the firm. So, with that coming fairly soon, I just decided to get myself a little something, something"

The girls were looking over the menu trying to decide what to have when a handsome waiter approached their table. He stood there for what seemed like a full five minutes without saying a word. Brook and Mia just looked at each other with confusion stamped all across their faces. Finally, Mr. Waiter Man decided to speak.

"Welcome to Harriston's ladies. I'm Colin and I'll be your server tonight. Your previous server had an emergency so I'm taking over. What can I get for you?"

Mia could feel her heart flutter. The man looked incredible and his baritone voice was the icing on the cake. Mia had always been a sucker for a tall, chocolate man with the physique of a Greek god. Hell, who wouldn't be a sucker for that? Mia was snapped out of her trance by the reply she heard coming from Brook's mouth.

"I'd be happy to give you my order Colin, if you can tell me why you stood here so long before deciding to speak."

"Oh, I was just gathering my thoughts, trying to regain my composure. I totally lost it when I realized that the two most beautiful women I'd ever seen were sitting at this table."

"Gee, I bet you say that to all the girls."

Mia was still just sitting there trying to find the right words so that she could join this little conversation.

"No, Brook, I bet he saved that line just for us...didn't you Colin?"

"That's right gorgeous, just for you."

Brook cleared her throat and giggled, "Ooh it's getting hot up in here. Colin I'll have an Apple Martini and if you'll excuse me I'm going to the ladies room. You two behave now." Brook made her exit and as she looked back over her shoulder she saw that Colin had actually taken her seat in front of Mia. Maybe this will be Mia's Mr. Right or at least Mr. Right Now.

Brook made her way back to the table and couldn't help but notice the silly school girl grin on Mia's face.

"Well dang, don't you look happy!"

"Girl, maybe I just found something to be happy about. That is one fine man and he's actually taller than me...even with my heels on. That alone makes me happy. I'm so tired of all these short men trying to get play from me."

"You shouldn't be so gorgeous."

"Yeah right, moving on. I did give him my number; we'll have to see if he actually calls."

"The way he was looking at you, I'm sure he'll be calling very soon."

Colin returned with their drinks and took their food orders. The girls sat there sharing good conversation and looking around at all the folks hanging out, trying to get their groove on. They laughed at the men dressed like modern day pimps and felt bad for the women in scantily clad outfits that could barely hold all of their body parts. It just didn't take all of that to get the attention of a man. And if it did, he's not a man that a self-respecting woman would want. Mia and Brook finished their meals, laughed a little while longer and then decided to call it a night. Colin was nice enough to escort the women to their car and gave Mia a gentle kiss good night...on the hand.

Once Mia and Brook arrived home, they each headed for their rooms to get showered and ready for bed. Once she was all dressed for bed, Brook decided to go to the kitchen and fix herself a relaxing cup of tea. Mia joined her for tea and a little more conversation.

"Brook, you never told me when you're going to start at the firm?"

"Oh, I thought I did. Monday after next will be my first day. I wanted to take another week or so because I'm scheduled to take the CPA exam next Tuesday. This gives me a few more days to study, I really want to go in there having passed the exam, you know what I mean?"

"I hear you girl, I hear you. Good for you!"

"Well Miss. Mia, I'm glad you're happy for me and I want to thank you so much for dinner tonight. It was great."

"No problem, I'm glad you enjoyed it. But now Brook, I'm going to turn in, I'm pretty tired and I have an early go in the morning."

"I hear you, I'm tired myself. Good night."

Brook had spent the last day and a half studying at home for the exam. She wanted to get a good amount of studying in before the weekend. Brook knew that this Saturday would be spent house hunting with Tameka. She was just getting up to fix herself some lunch when the phone rang.

"Hello"

"Hey girl, I need a favor."

"Hey Mia, what is it?"

"I'm supposed to meet Colin at the house at four o'clock; I may be running a couple of minutes late. If he gets there before I do, would you please let him in and offer him a drink? I shouldn't be any more than five or ten minutes late."

"Um, sure, but you don't think it's a little too soon to have him over? You just met him two days ago."

"Yeah, I know, but I've talked to him a lot and I've got a great feeling about him."

"Well, okay girlfriend, I'll be happy to let him in for you and even fix him a drink. You know me, Miss. Hospitality."

"Thank you very much and I'll see you a little later okay."

"Alright, bye."

Brook was glad that Mia had a good feeling about oh boy, he did seem very nice, but she still thought it was too soon to let him come over. You just can't trust everyone to know where you live. On Brook's second attempt to go fix some lunch the phone rang again.

"Hello"

"Hey Brook, it's me Tameka. Are you going to be home

later? I want to bring over these home listings we were talking about yesterday."

"Yeah, why not. I'm not getting too much accomplished right now anyway. What time will you be over?"

"Sometime around four. See you then, bye."

"Bye."

Okay, Brook thought to herself. Let's try this again. She moved towards the kitchen and stopped to look at the phone. It didn't ring so she felt safe to move on and get some food for her empty stomach.

Brook had fallen asleep on the couch and was in the middle of a dream when she was awakened by the doorbell. She thought that it must be Tameka with the home listings. She'd forgotten about Colin and was surprised to see him standing there.

"Oh Colin, I'd almost forgotten that you were coming over. Mia isn't here yet but please come on in."

"Brook, I hope I didn't disturb you."

"No, I was just stealing a little relaxation time. But I needed to get up anyway and get myself together."

"Huh, you look all together to me."

Brook looked at him out of the corner of her eye wondering what he meant by that. She chose to ignore his little comment and offered him something to drink.

"Brook, I'd love a glass of wine if you'll have one with me."

"Oh no, I'll pass, but I'll get you some. White or red?"

"Never mind the wine, why don't you just come and sit and talk with me until Mia arrives?"

This whole situation was starting to make Brook very uncomfortable. She wondered what the hell was taking Mia so long. "Well, you can talk but I'll be in the kitchen cleaning up." As Brook stood at the sink, Colin came up behind her and wrapped his arms around her waist. Brook jumped and pushed him away from her.

"What the hell is wrong with you? Get away from me!"

"Brook please, I could tell by the way you looked at me the

other night that you wanted me so don't trip now. Just go with it."

"Don't you know that Mia will be here in a minute, you idiot?"

"If you cooperate, we can work fast and both enjoy the ride."

"Negro please, you need to go. Get the hell out!"

Brook stepped past him to go to the door when he suddenly grabbed her hand. Brook snatched it away, ran and threw the front door open. He walked to the door and slammed it shut. Without hesitation Brook went for the phone to call 911 and without hesitation he knocked it out of her hand. "You bitches really can be silly. Did you really think I'd let you call the cops on me?" Brook was now at a loss and just decided to jet for the door. Colin cut her off at the pass and grabbed her around the waist. In one swoop he had Brook bent over the back of the couch and was trying to unfasten her pants. Brook managed to free a knee and brought it up as strong as she could between this ass' legs. She actually felt a rush of success as he squealed like a pig and bent over in pain. Brook ran for the door again but he tripped her and instantly straddled her on the floor smacking her with his closed fist right across the cheek.

"Why are you pretending to be this sweet little thing when you know that you want this so bad. Just stop fighting and go with it, cause if you don't, one of us will get hurt and it won't be me."

Brook started trying to fight with all that she had and screaming at the top of her lungs and once again she was smacked in the face, but she continued her fight. Suddenly the front door flew open and Brook heard a crash and then an unbelievably heavy weight on her body. She then felt free as Tameka rolled Colin off of her body.

"Brook, are you alright? Who is this ass? Let me call the cops!"

"Tameka, thank God you came. Is he dead?"

"Hell no, his ass ain't dead, but he needs to be. Who the hell is he?"

"Mia's new friend, he was supposed to meet her here but she was running late. Are you sure he isn't dead?"

"Girl please, he's just out cold, the police are on the way. Are you okay, did he umm, I mean did he umm…rape you?" Tameka asked as gently as she could while holding Brook in her arms.

"No, he'd just hit me when you clocked him with that lamp. I don't know how to thank you, you really saved me and I won't forget it."

# CHAPTER EIGHT

Brook got up the next morning and began to get herself ready for a day of house hunting. She looked in the mirror to see if applying makeup would even help her appearance. Those licks she took yesterday had left a couple of ugly bruises. She put on a little eye liner, foundation and lipstick anyway, God knows it couldn't hurt. Brook took another glance in the mirror and headed for the kitchen. Mia entered the kitchen slowly as Brook sat at the table with a cup of coffee. Mia took a seat across from Brook and looked up with tears in her eyes.

"Brook, I couldn't sleep at all last night. I am so sorry for allowing him in this house, for putting you in that situation, for my bad judgment. I feel so stupid and like such a sorry friend. I don't know how to make it up to you."

"Mia, you are not a sorry friend, you are my best friend and I still love you. You have nothing to make up to me, you've already been too good to me."

"How can you say that, you are the one that said it was too soon to allow Colin over here in the first place?"

"I can say that because we both know that you had no control over what that idiot would do. You are not psychic.

You've opened your home and your heart to me and I couldn't ask for a better sister."

"Well, thank you for saying that, I just hope you really mean it."

"Of course I do, you know I don't lie." Brook said with a smile as she reached out and squeezed Mia's hand.

The girls sat there in silence for a while and enjoyed their coffee and the morning paper. Mia put her paper down and cleared her throat as she prepared to ask Brook a couple of questions about her living arrangements.

"Brook, are you still seriously considering letting Tameka live with you when you move?"

"Um yeah, I think it might really work out. Besides, this is a chance for me to show my appreciation for what she did yesterday."

"Please don't do this out of some sense of duty or repayment to her, any friend would have done the same thing."

"I realize that, but we were going to move in together anyway and this all just confirms my decision. But don't worry, I had my attorney draw up a great lease that gives me all the benefits and say so over my home, living conditions, her payments to me and control over a quick eviction if the need ever arises."

"I just want you to be sure…don't let her guilt or pressure you into this."

"Don't worry, I'm in complete control and comfortable with this situation. But thank you for worrying about me."

Brook was clearing her things from the table when the doorbell rang. She went and let Tameka in, they had decided to ride together today and just follow Lauren from house to house.

"Good morning Tameka, come on in and let me get my bag and jacket, I'll be right back."

Mia walked into the living room and greeted Tameka with a stiff smile but pleasant hello. The two of them just stood around in silence for a minute when Mia just couldn't hold her tongue any longer.

"So Tameka, are you sure you want a roommate? Wouldn't you prefer a place of your own with all the space and privacy a grown woman needs?"

"Well, aren't you just all concerned about me and what I need? Oh no, of course you aren't, you're worried about Brook and what I may do to her. Just know that I will never put her in the danger you put her in yesterday. To be such a good friend you sure show poor judgment. Next time why don't you just hire an ax murderer to come in and knock her off?"

"Damn it, that's enough!" screamed Brook as she re-entered the room. "Can ya'll be civil to each other for at least 30 seconds? I swear this is so damn ridiculous it's not even funny!"

"Brook, you know I love you and that I'm just trying to look out for your best interest."

"Well Mia, I am a grown woman, I love you too but I can manage my own life."

"Well I guess you heard that…"

"Tameka, shut up and let's go!"

Brook and Tameka left Mia standing in the middle of the living room floor. That little talk hadn't gone at all the way she'd wanted it to.

It was a beautiful, cool, crisp morning. The trees were all shedding their colorful leaves and the grass was beginning to turn brown. Brook was glad she wasn't driving, but instead able to sit on the passenger side and take in her surroundings. She took in a deep breath as if to cleanse herself of any bad vibes left by earlier conflicts. She wanted that cleansing breath to fill her with a happy, peaceful feeling. Deep down she knew she was looking to be filled with the spirit of God. She'd just really realized how long it had been since she had gone to church, listened to her favorite gospel music or even prayed the deep prayers she'd done so often. She still prayed every night but the prayers that were so deep that she'd choke on her tears and be filled with a spirit that stayed with her for days had sadly fallen by the wayside. She wanted them back, she needed them back in her life.

"Are you okay over there? Haven't said anything for a while." Tameka's words jerked Brook out of her meditative like state. Brook did a double take not realizing that they had traveled to Grady Homes housing project.

"Are we going to see your mom?" Brook asked in a confused voice.

"No, my brother lives around the corner and since we still have about twenty minutes before we meet Lauren, I thought I'd take the chance that he'd be home. I hope you don't mind, but I just need him to do a little favor for me."

Tameka didn't bother to say what the favor was, that was better left between her and her baby brother.

"No, I don't mind, just as long as we're on time to meet Lauren. By the way, why haven't I met your brother before?"

Tameka giggled, "Girl he's in and out of jail so much I'm lucky to ever see him my damn self. He's a nice guy but nobody's angel."

Brook just shrugged her shoulders as Tameka pulled into a parking spot. Tameka didn't bother to get out of the car; she just picked up her cell phone and dialed his number. A couple of minutes later this young man with a baby face and fine body glided over to the car. Tameka let the window down and introduced Brook to her brother Derrick. She then let the window back up, got out of the car and advised Brook that she'd only be a minute. Brook sat in the car and found a gospel station on the radio while Tameka told her brother a little story about a guy named Craig.

Brook and Tameka pulled up into a town house community right behind Lauren. Their timing couldn't have been better. Lauren got out of her car looking like a breath of fresh air. She and Brook hugged and then she politely spoke to Tameka. Brook couldn't help but ask what was giving Lauren that extra little spring in her step. Lauren's face lit up even brighter as she held out her left hand.

"After the concert last night, my man asked for my hand in marriage and I happily said yes. I guess I'm still floating on that cloud called love," Lauren said with a giggle.

Brook grabbed Lauren and gave her a big hug. "I'm so happy for you, this is so great! Do you have a date in mind?"

Before she could answer Tameka reached her hand out to shake Laurens and gave her what appeared to be a sincere congratulation. Lauren smiled and was surprised by Tameka's efforts at sincerity.

"Well thank you Tameka and as far as a date, Peter wants to tie the knot ASAP, but it looks like it will be around February. I've got to have a minute to pull something decent together."

The ladies moved on from the parking lot to begin their day of house hunting. The first condo they looked at was just one of seven houses they would see before the day was over. There was one in particular that Brook absolutely loved and Tameka thought was great but not her first choice. Lauren suggested that they stop for a bite to eat and discuss the houses they'd seen. Over coffee and dessert Brook decided she wanted to go back and put a contract on the house she adored. Two hours later Brook walked in the door of Mia's house with contract in hand for the purchase of her own home. Now it was her turn to walk on the clouds.

# CHAPTER NINE

It had been three weeks and Brook was set to close on her new home. She was enjoying her new job and was so pleased with herself that she'd managed to pass the CPA exam. She felt accomplished that she'd been able to demand a higher salary based on her new professional status. It wasn't the money that made her feel good, but the fact that she had passed the exam the first time around and was actually moving her life in a positive direction. There was only one other thing she had to do that would make her feel complete, and that was going back to church. With that in mind, Brook put the finishing touches on her makeup and double checked her outfit in the mirror. She was pleased with what she saw, so she grabbed her purse and walked out of her room.

Mia was lounging on the couch when Brook walked into the family room and asked her if she wanted to go to church with her. Mia sat up, looked at Brook and laid back down. "I think I'll pass."

Brook went over and sat at Mia's feet. "Mia sweetie, are you okay? You've been acting so funny lately, is everything alright?"

Mia sat up on the couch and looked Brook square in the eyes. Mia's face was completely wet with tears.

"I thought I was ready for you to leave, you know, move out. But without you here I'll truly be alone again. I'm so lonely right now. I have been for a while but at least you were here and I didn't have to sit by myself all day and night. There is something missing and I feel that with you gone the hole in my life will only get bigger."

As Mia broke down crying, Brook held her tight in her arms and tried to console her. They didn't speak for ten whole minutes; they just sat there and held on to one another. Brook had always understood the power of silence. Sometimes you just needed to be held, to know without words that you are loved. When they finally pulled away, Brook wiped Mia's face, kissed her cheek and insisted that they both go to church.

The ladies stood for the Benediction, picked up their hand bags and eased out of the aisle. This service had done them both a world of good. The singing, the sermon, it was all amazing. As they approached Brook's car they heard someone running up behind them. The most appealing voice called out "Excuse me, aren't you Brook?" Brook and Mia both turned to see the man that belonged to the voice and what a man he was. Tall, handsome and fine.

"Hi, Brook, I don't know if you remember me or not but my name is Eric Banks. We met briefly one night at Dailey's."

Eric's words seemed to flow out of his mouth as smoothly as water flows down a stream. Brook hesitated briefly and replied, "I'm sorry I don't remember, I must not have been myself that night." She was now fidgeting, looking in her purse for her sunglasses. This Eric made Brook a little nervous, a little unsure of herself. How in the world could she have forgotten this man?

"Well, I didn't want to hold you up, but I did want to just remind you of me. Please, take my card and give me a call sometime. I promise that I'm a good guy. I work hard and do pretty well for myself. I'm not a stalker. I…I just couldn't believe my luck seeing you again and couldn't let you leave without speaking. You're so beautiful and I can only imagine that you must be as equally interesting. I know I'm rambling, so I'll let you ladies go. Please, have a blessed day and call me sometime. Bye."

Eric walked away feeling foolish. As he approached his car he heard someone call his name. "Eric, wait a minute." Brook called out as she made her way to his car.

"Please forgive me for my rudeness, for just standing there without responding. You seem like a lovely person but I'm just a little gun shy right now. I don't want to offer any encouragement when I know that I'm not looking to get involved with anyone."

Eric looked at her with a puzzled expression, "who said I wanted to get involved?"

Brook looked surprised and a little deflated. "Well, don't I feel a little foolish."

The look on Eric's face changed and he began to laugh lightly. He bent his knees so that he and Brook could be face to face.

"I was only kidding, just teasing you. Please don't feel foolish. I wouldn't want to make you feel anything but happy."

Brook's face eased into a warm smile before she even realized it. And then she remembered Mia.

"Oh my goodness, we've just been talking and my friend is just standing there by herself. I've got to go."

Brook turned to walk away when Eric suggested he walk her back to her car. Brook looked at Mia and very sincerely apologized for her rudeness. Needless to say that Mia wasn't the least bit upset. She figured that if she couldn't find a man that was her problem, but wouldn't begrudge Brook any happiness that she might find.

"Ladies, I don't know about you two but I'm starving. Can I interest you in a little brunch? You guys can follow me in your car and I promise it will be the best food you've had in a long time."

Not wanting to give Brook the chance to say no, Mia immediately answered "Why yes, Eric, we'd love to join you. Just lead the way." Brook smiled politely and agreed to go.

Mia, Brook and Eric enjoyed light hearted conversation, excellent lobster tail and mimosas. Brook had to admit to herself that this guy was more than a pretty face. He was intelligent, humorous and seemed to be very kind. But she still wasn't ready to let herself get involved.

After Eric paid the check he walked the ladies back to Brook's car. "Thank you so much for sharing a meal with me, I couldn't have asked for better company."

Mia smiled and thanked Eric and used the cold weather as an excuse for getting into the car.

Brook looked at Eric very sweetly, "Thank you for brunch, it was delicious."

Eric smiled at Brook and took her hand in his. "I know that you're not looking to get involved and I respect that. "You have my number, all three of them," he said with a chuckle. He gently but firmly squeezed Brook's hand and then he asked if they knew their way from the restaurant. Once he knew they were okay to get home, he stroked the back of Brooks hand, gently let it go and walked away.

As Brook drove down the street in silence, she looked around and soaked up the atmosphere. It was cold, but sunny and clear. Fall was in full swing, one might even think that winter had arrived. As she continued to drive and survey her surroundings, she caught a glimpse of Mia out of the corner of her eye. Mia was staring at her very intently.

"What?"

"Nothing."

"There is some reason you're staring me down like I'm the last chicken wing on the buffet."

"I can't figure out why you're just over there looking all happy-go-lucky when you know I'm dying to know what was said between you and Eric."

"Oh, is that why you're looking so crazy? All you had to do was ask."

"Alright funny lady, just spill the beans."

THE KNIFE IN MY BACK    47

Brook sat there for a moment in silence contemplating how she would relay the conversation. She didn't want to let on that she may really be interested in this guy.

"Well, he said that he couldn't let me leave without reminding me of him and that he thought I was beautiful. He said he understood that I wasn't looking to get involved but that I had his numbers and could call if I wanted. That about sums it up."

"And why does he think you're not looking to be involved?"

"Because I told him."

"And why tell him that?"

"Because I don't think I'm ready."

"And why not?"

"Mia, if you ask me why just one more time I'm going to put you out of my car."

"Ooh, testy. That comment almost makes you sound as if you're more interested than you let on."

"No, Mia, that comment makes it sound as if I'm tired of you asking me why."

Mia sat quiet for a moment, contemplating Brook and her reasons for thinking she wasn't ready for a relationship. Brook hadn't really dated anyone since the first semester of her senior year, which was just about a year ago. There was absolutely no reason for her to subject herself to a life of loneliness.

"Brook, you do realize that you've lost your parents and not your spouse."

"I'm very aware of that, but getting involved means letting down your guard and that opens you up to the possibility of being hurt. I don't want any more hurt in my life."

"I can understand that, but if you don't open yourself up, you not only won't get hurt, but you won't experience any joy. You remember Thomas right?"

"Yeah, the great love of your life. I also remember how he hurt you."

"I remember the hurt too. But Brook, the ride with him was

worth the fall. I did hurt for a while but I also had the time of my life for a while. I wouldn't trade it. I'm still open to the possibility of feeling that way about someone else because I know that I deserve to be loved. Your parents would also want for you to experience the love that they shared with one another."

"Well, seems like you've given me a little something to marinade on."

# CHAPTER TEN

Tameka looked around her room and smiled. This was the last time she'd ever have to look at this depressing place and know that it's where she'd have to lay her head. She had packed up and moved everything out already, she just wanted to pick up the last bag of shoes she had forgotten on her previous moving day. Brook had closed on the condo a month earlier and after two weeks of trying to persuade her differently, Tameka finally gave up and signed the lease Brook had drawn up. She knew that someone else had to talk her into doing the lease in the first place. Tameka didn't give Brook enough credit; she just couldn't believe that Brook had the guts or common sense to come up with the lease idea on her own. Tameka still viewed Brook as the sweet little naive rich girl. But at any rate, the lease was signed and she was moving into one of the most upscale condos that Atlanta had to offer.

After putting the remainder of her things in the car, Tameka re-entered her mom's house ready to sit and share the dinner that had been prepared. As she reached to get a plate, she realized that there were two things she would miss, her mom and that delicious home cooking.

"Mom, everything smells so good. I can't remember the last

time you fixed salmon croquettes and fried potatoes with onion. I hope I can refrain from making a pig of myself."

"Child please, you eat like a bird. It would be nice to see you just let go and eat til you get tired. It would do my heart good."

"Well Mom, you know that a diva like me has to watch her figure. The boys don't come running after fat cows."

"You ought to be ashamed of yourself."

"Hey, I'm just speaking the truth. The truth is the light," Tameka said with laughter in her voice.

"Child, hush you mouth and turn the news up before you sit down with that plate."

They sat in silence as they ate and listened to the 6:00 news. It was amazing the horrible things people did to one another on a daily basis. Murder, rape, assault, drugs, it was all just about more than Ms. Williams could stand. She felt that they had to be living in the last days.

"Mom, do you see the way she holds her mouth when she speaks? It almost looks as if she's had a stroke. I can't believe that she's the lead anchor for this prime time slot. What in the world did she have to do to get this job?"

"Don't you think that was kinda mean? How could you even be thinking about the way she looks when they just finished talking about a double murder?"

"Mama, people get killed every day. I have to pay attention to the way people look and how they deliver the news, it's part of my job. Besides, I have to sum up the competition and make sure I'm better if I want to move to anchor over at CNN."

"Baby, you're going to be the anchor? That's wonderful."

"Yeah, I'm gonna be the anchor, they just don't know it yet."

"Oh well, I guess you have to think big. It's always good to set a goal and start working towards it."

Tameka decided to drop that subject because she knew that her mom would never approve of her ideas on how to achieve this current goal. She would never understand the importance of the anchor position for Tameka. Producer was cool, it was a good job that a lot of people would love to have. But Tameka longed to be in the lime light, she wanted to be seen and for everyone to know her name. She didn't want to be just another person working behind the scenes. All she had to do was figure out how to get on air just one time. One time was all she would need to make a strong impression and leave the powers that be wanting her up front for good.

"Have you talked to your brother lately?"

"Huh? What did you say?"

"I asked if you've heard from your brother lately?"

"Oh, I talked to him a couple of weeks ago. I actually stopped by to see him about a month ago. You know, just to make sure he's doing okay and staying out of trouble."

"Well, is he staying out of trouble? The last thing that boy needs is to get locked up again. You'd think that after a while he'd get tired of sleeping in a cell with a bunch of men."

"I don't know Mom, I try to talk to him, but you know he doesn't listen to me."

Tameka almost couldn't believe the things she heard coming out of her own mouth. Her mom would have a heart attack if she knew that Tameka asked her brother to do something illegal, to physically harm another person. But Tameka truly felt that the bastard deserved to be hurt. No one treats her the way Craig did and gets off scot free. It just didn't work that way in the world of Tameka. She never thought that she had any ownership in the way things happened. One day she'd learn that you can't treat people just any old way.

"So, when do I get to see this beautiful new place of yours and Brooks?"

"Well Mom, as a matter of fact, we were considering having a nice big Christmas dinner. Wouldn't that be nice?"

"Yeah, but I was thinking you'd ask me to ride over there with you today. I just want to know where you're living."

"And you will…at Christmas. I want everything to be in place and looking good when you first see it."

"If you say so. I just thought that maybe I could help ya'll get it together. Help you put things away and decorate."

"We've got it under control Mom. I just want it to be perfect when you see it."

Tameka got up from the table and took their plates and glasses to the sink. She stayed long enough to clean up the kitchen and share a little more small talk with her mom. Before leaving, Tameka wrote her mom a check for five hundred dollars and gave a her big hug and kiss.

"I love you, Mama. If you need anything before I get back over here just call me."

Tameka turned and left. She was so excited to be going to her new home, the kind of home she felt she'd always deserved. It was now her turn to come up in the world. New home today, lead anchor tomorrow and who knows what else was in her future. A new man wouldn't hurt, she thought to herself. A new man with plenty of money and good benefits. Brook had told her about the guy she and Mia had brunch with after church a few weeks ago. He sounded fabulous but if she wanted to hold onto that condo she'd better leave Brook's friend alone. Maybe he had a friend.

Tameka made her way through the city, soaking up all the sights as if it were the first time she'd ever been there. She felt almost giddy as she turned the corner and pulled out her security card to gain entrance into the parking garage.

"Hello Miss Williams, how are you today?"

"I'm fine thank you."

She couldn't believe that Jeffery, the doorman, already knew her name. This was the life, she couldn't imagine it getting much better than this. She was almost letting herself lose perspective on whose home this really was.

# CHAPTER ELEVEN

Lunch rush at Houston's was no joke. Brook and Mia decided to head over at 11:30 in an effort to get ahead of some of the crowd. Brook enjoyed the food okay, but Mia was absolutely mad for their apple walnut crisp desert. It was so cute the way Mia ate like a bird with just a small side salad and then pigged out on that cobbler thing. That's why Brook never put up an argument when Mia suggested Houston's for lunch. Anything for a friend.

"So, how is the decorator working out for you? Are your tastes compatible?"

"Girl, she is fabulous. Costly, but well worth the price. As a matter of fact, the place is almost complete."

"That sounds great! Is she also doing Tameka's room or is that area off limits?"

The waiter interrupted the conversation by placing their food on the table. Mia had her usual side salad while Brook decided to indulge in the salmon.

"Believe it or not, Tameka did get some input from the decorator on her room as well. They butted heads a couple of times but her room is really coming together nicely. Now you know she wanted more say so in the decorating of the rest of the place."

"Did you let her put her two cents in?"

"Well, I did listen to her ideas and suggestions, actually implemented a couple of them. I just wanted her to feel like it was her home too, but that's as far as I allowed her input to go."

"I feel you. After all, it is your home. She's just temporary."

"Oh, be nice. For now it's her home too."

"Whatever."

"Well how about we just change the subject. You are going to be at the house for Christmas dinner, right?"

"Absolutely, wouldn't miss spending the holiday with you for the world. Besides, my folks decided to travel this year and I don't want to cramp the love bird's style."

"Where are they going?"

"Well, Mom has always dreamed of Paris. Girl, the woman's got snow globes, booklets and everything else on that place. So Daddy finally saved enough for them to make the trip. Needless to say, this trip is her gift."

"That is so sweet. My mom loved Paris too. But hey girl, we will have a fabulous time right here in Hotlanta!"

"Brook, have you decided if you're going to spend any of the holidays in Baltimore with family?"

"I actually have a round trip ticket for the weekend after next. I'll spend the night, make the rounds to my aunties and uncles homes and end my trip by visiting the cemetery. Girl, I can't believe I'm spending Christmas without my parents. It's just so unreal."

"I can only imagine how strange and difficult it must be for you."

"Well, this is obviously the way God intended. It's time for me to blaze my own trail and keep moving in a positive direction. God is good to me girl, I've gained so much strength through Him since I've started back with church and the talks and prayers I share with my God. I realize now that my parents would want me to move on. It finally hit me that moving on doesn't mean forgetting them, it just means that I have to continue to live and hey, I can still make them proud of me."

"I'm so glad to hear you talk like this and trust me, if you won the Nobel Peace Prize your parents couldn't be any more proud of you."

"Oh, you're gonna make me cry."

"Child please, that is not my goal."

The waiter brought the check and Brook immediately gave him her platinum credit card. She then pulled out a hand mirror and lipstick and gave herself a quick touch up. The waiter returned with her card and receipts, she added on a generous tip and signed her name.

"Thank you for lunch but you didn't have to do that."

"I know that. Are you ready to head back to the office?"

"Ready when you are, sweetie."

The girls grabbed their bags and headed out of the restaurant. Fifteen minutes later Brook pulled into a parking space near the entrance of their building. Then they just sat there and looked at one another, neither of them were ready to get back to work. Brook was always excited around the holidays and this year was no different. Even though she wouldn't be with her parents, she was still happy to be spending this Christmas in her new home with her wonderful friends.

"You know we can't sit here much longer." Mia stated, interrupting Brooks train of thought.

"Yeah, I know. You ready to head in?'

"Yes ma'am, but I want to ask you something first."

"Shoot."

"Wouldn't you like to invite Eric over for Christmas dinner? I'm sure he'd love to spend his holiday with you. The poor guy gladly accepts any time he can get with you, which up to now has only been a few lunch dates."

"We talk on the phone a lot. Doesn't that count for something?'

"Not for much, it's nothing like spending time face to face. Ma bell only gets you so far."

"But I'm sure he'll be with his family, he probably already has plans."

"You'll never know until you ask Brook. You know you like the man, I mean hell, what's not to like. Give yourself a great Christmas present by letting Eric be the one sitting by your side at dinner."

"I just don't want to be disappointed if he says no."

"I get a strong feeling that he won't say no."

The next morning as Brook tried to focus on her work, she just couldn't keep her mind from drifting to Eric. She wouldn't admit her true feelings to anyone because that would make them too real. She wouldn't admit that she thought of him constantly and was being more drawn to him with every phone conversation and every lunch date. But now Mia wanted her to step it up a notch and ask him to Christmas dinner. This was a huge deal to Brook because rejection of her invitation would truly crush her. Brook was not accustomed to rejection and didn't want to have it become part of her life now. Then, suddenly and without hesitation, Brook picked up the phone and dialed Eric's work number.

"Ackerman, Hayes and Associates, how may I direct your call?"

"Mr. Eric Banks, please?"

"One moment."

Brook held the phone wondering if she should even be making this call.

"Eric Banks speaking."

"Hi Eric, this is Brook. I hope that I'm not disturbing you."

"Miss Mansfield, you can disturb me any time. I was actually sitting here thinking of you. How are you today?"

"I'm just peachy, how are you?"

"Well I'm great now. Were you calling for a specific reason or because you missed me? Hopefully because you missed me."

"Actually, I was calling to invite you over for Christmas dinner. I completely understand if you already have plans, I just thought I'd extend the invitation."

"Wow, thank you for the invite. I'll be happy to give you my answer over dinner tonight. What do you say?"

"Um, dinner…tonight?"

"We both have to eat, why not eat together. We seem to enjoy each others company at lunch, why not make it a real date?"

"Sure, why not. Where do you want to meet?"

This was more than Brook had bargained for. She wasn't prepared for a real date, wasn't at all sure that she'd be comfortable in an intimate setting. Was this going to be his way of gently saying no to her Christmas invitation? God knows she didn't want to be rejected.

# CHAPTER TWELVE

Tameka strolled into work a few minutes early. She made her way to the break room to get some coffee. A little jolt of caffeine would do her some good right now. Everyone knew that she was not a morning person so anything to help her shake that early funk was welcome. What was not welcome was that damn chipper, happy-go-lucky Monica Greer, noon day anchor extraordinaire. But here she was heading in Tameka's direction, grinning ear to ear. Tameka thought to herself, "doesn't this idiot know that she's just not that good? If not for my direction she'd just sit in that anchor chair day after day looking like a dumb monkey." She knew that if given the opportunity she'd be so much better in that chair.

"Good morning Tameka. How are you today? Ready to work through the top stories for today?"

"Morning to you too, Monica. I'm going to head to my office and start sorting through everything that's coming in and I'll get with you in a little while."

"Not in a good mood? Did you wake up on the wrong side of the bed sweetie?"

"Whatever, Monica."

"Well, wait a minute, Tameka; have you heard anything from Craig lately?"

"Why would you think I've heard from him, do I look like his keeper?"

"Excuse me; all of that attitude is not even necessary. I only asked because no one around here has seen or heard from him in three days. He hasn't called into work or anything. His manager is contemplating filing a missing person's report."

Monica turned and headed out of the room, but right before she walked out of the door, she turned to Tameka and shot daggers with her eyes. "It really wasn't necessary for you to speak to me so harshly, Tameka. I can't help it if something is wrong with you and if there is, I did nothing to contribute to the problem, learn how to treat people!" Monica then left the room and continued on with her day as if she'd never had words with Tameka.

Angry with the knowledge that Monica felt it was okay to speak to her in that manner, Tameka entered her office and slammed the door. That bitch was completely out of line. Freaking Monica Greer, can barely read copy without stumbling over her words, let alone a teleprompter. Tameka could understand if she really had been harsh with Monica, but all she did was answer her damn questions. Oh yeah, her last question, where could poor little Craig be? She sat down at her desk and picked up the phone. As she dialed her brothers number she prayed that he was home.

"Hello"

"Derrick, is that you?"

"No, hold on a minute."

Tameka tapped her pen on the desk as she waited for her brother to pick up the phone.

"Hello"

"Derrick, who was that hoodlum that just answered the phone?"

"Just one of my boys. What's up baby girl?"

"A co-worker just told me that Craig hasn't been heard from in about three days. Know anything about it?"

"I know you ain't asking me this shit on the phone! Are you crazy?"

"I just wanted to know..."

"Girl all you need to know is that anything you ask me to do for you I try to do. Bye!"

Just like that Derrick had hung up the phone leaving Tameka with more questions than she originally had. If her brother had gotten Craig for disrespecting her, how had he done it? Was Craig dead or just hurt really bad? Tameka wanted to know every single detail. Why had she promised to take Brook to the airport after work? All she wanted to do now was to see her brother, but she knew that by the time she made it back from the airport, Derrick would be long gone for the night.

Tameka hated driving in the rain and it was just her luck that it had started to drizzle when she pulled out of the parking garage. Folks in Atlanta already couldn't drive and they just seem to really lose their minds in the rain. It seemed that bad weather encouraged them to drive their absolute worse. Needless to say, Tameka breathed a sigh of relief once she pulled safely in front of her building. Brook was waiting in the lobby with her bags and when the doorman saw Tameka's car, he immediately escorted Brook out with an umbrella and placed her bags in the trunk. Brook tipped him and she and Tameka pulled off.

"Well girl, are you ready for this trip?"

"As ready as I'm ever going to be. I really appreciate your taking me to the airport."

"No problem. Do all of your folks know you're on your way?"

"I called all my aunties and uncles; they know I'll be in tonight. What they don't know is that I'm leaving right back out tomorrow evening."

"Why did you decide to only stay overnight? I would've thought you would want more time with your family."

"I don't know, it just doesn't feel the same. I want to see everyone and let them see that I'm actually doing okay, but after that, I just don't see the point. It doesn't feel like my home anymore."

"I guess I can understand that."

"So, what are your plans for the night?"

"This guy I met a while back is taking me out to dinner."

"Sounds good, what's his name and why are you holding out on the juicy information?"

"Child please, there's nothing juicy about this. His name is Wayne and we met when he came by the TV station for a business meeting. He's pretty nice but in all honestly, I just need a tune up."

"What do you mean a tune up? I know you're not going to have this man working on your car."

"Brook, I really wonder about you sometimes. By tune up I mean sex. I haven't had it in a while and my body is in need."

"I knew what you meant; I just wanted you to break it down."

"Yeah right."

Tameka headed the car toward the south terminal and slowly pulled up to Brooks airline. She popped the trunk and jumped out of the car as Brook got out on her side. Tameka gave Brook her bags and a warm hug. Brook hugged her back and warned Tameka to be careful going home and to use protection while being tuned up. Tameka watched as Brook disappeared beyond the sliding doors and a police officer blew his whistle at Tameka signaling her to move her car.

As Tameka drove through the city streets she decided to try her brother again from her cell phone. Just as she'd figured, he was long gone. She dropped her phone in her purse and started contemplating what she would wear tonight. She couldn't believe that after the rough day she'd had, there was actually something to look forward to tonight. Wayne was a tall, dark brother with hazel eyes and soft, curly hair. He had a cut body that was proof positive that exercise does work. So it was Tameka's plan tonight to leave him with an unshakeable image of her. She was impressed with his looks, but now it was her job to leave him impressed with not only her appearance, but her mind and her moves. The kind of moves that makes a grown man cry for more like a baby cries for his bottle.

Tameka glided through the doors of Sambuca's Jazz Café looking like a runway model. She wore a black Donna Karen dress that fit every curve of her body like a glove. Her beautiful legs were accented by a pair of three inch pumps. She could feel all eyes on her as the hostess escorted her to the table where Wayne was patiently waiting.

"Good evening, I hope I haven't kept you waiting too long."

"Sweetheart, you are definitely worth the wait," Wayne said as he stood to greet Tameka and help with her chair.

"Well thank you. What are you drinking?'

"This is just club soda, but how about we kick it up a notch and have a bottle of champagne?"

"That sounds fabulous."

The waiter came and took their drink order and went over the nights menu with them. They placed their food orders and then turned their attention to the band. The front man was an excellent saxophonist and Tameka allowed herself to get caught up in his rapture. She's not sure how much time had passed before she realized that Wayne had obviously gotten caught up in her. He was staring at her so intently that it almost made her uncomfortable...almost.

"So, Wayne, tell me, why are you looking at me like that?"

"I can't help it, you are so damn gorgeous that nothing else in here is worth looking at."

"You sure know how to flatter a girl."

"Oh baby, you haven't seen anything yet. I can do a whole lot more than just flatter you."

"And what do you mean by that?"

"Let's just say that if given the chance, I will treat you like a princess and make

you feel as if your body were a sexual nerve waiting to explode."

They both immediately burst into laughter.

"That was corny as hell wasn't it?"

"Yes, Wayne, that would rank among the top ten weakest lines."

"What can I say, I'm no Casanova. I guess I was trying to say that I would work hard to make you happy and do whatever it takes to please you if you'd give me the chance."

"Now that was sweet."

The waiter returned with their food, but before digging in, they lifted their glasses in a toast to a wonderful evening. They ate the excellent food that was spread out before them and shared great conversation. This date was turning out better than either had actually expected. Tameka was just really looking for a tune up but this guy seemed to be someone she might really be able to get into. After finishing dinner they decided to head to Wayne's place for coffee. Tameka followed Wayne in her car contemplating just how far she'd let things go tonight. He seemed like such a good guy and she didn't want to ruin a potential relationship by giving up the goodies too soon. But she ultimately decided to just go with the flow and let the night play itself out. She would follow wherever it led.

Tameka felt very comfortable in Wayne's home. He had a nicely decorated three bedroom home that felt safe and warm. While he was in the kitchen making coffee she made herself more comfortable by kicking off her shoes and looking through his DVD collection.

"Did you find anything you'd like to see?" Wayne asked as he sat the coffee tray down on the table in front of them.

"Not really, why don't you pick something?"

"Okay, I pick music over movie, is that okay with you?"

"Oh yeah, that's fine."

They sat there drinking coffee, listening to music and gazing at one another. Just as Tameka was getting ready to speak, Wayne leaned in and gently kissed her. He quickly went from gentle pecks to deep, passionate kisses. As he stroked Tameka's hair and face, she could feel her breath quicken. He pulled her even closer and began to kiss her neck and caress her body. It took every ounce of strength Tameka had in her body to pull away.

"Maybe we are moving too fast."

"Is that how you really feel or do you think it's the lady like thing to say because believe me, no matter how far we go, I know you're a lady and will respect you as such."

"Do you have any condoms?"

"I've got you baby; just let me take care of you."

Wayne stood to his feet and pulled Tameka to hers. He then led her down the hall to the master bedroom. He lit a couple of candles and turned his attention back to Tameka. Wayne began to kiss her with such passion that she was immediately excited. He unzipped her dress, let it drop to the floor and immediately cupped her full breasts in his hands. Tameka could hardly contain herself and began to rip at the buttons on his shirt. He took over and removed his shirt and pants and lifted Tameka off her feet allowing her to rap her legs around his waist. He turned around and gently laid her on the bed and began to kiss her mouth and make his way down her body with his tongue. He paused at her breasts, sucking them firmly causing Tameka to moan with pleasure. He moved further down her body to that special place that made her know that she was being loved. He kissed, licked and sucked her to her first orgasm of the night. By the time they Finished, Tameka was more satisfied than she had ever been and Wayne thought he was in love.

# CHAPTER THIRTEEN

Brook moved around the house as if she were running a marathon. Tameka stopped what she was doing and just stood back and watched her. Brook wasn't getting much accomplished because she would stop one task to start another and never make it back to the original job. Tameka couldn't understand why Brook was so frantic over Christmas. It was just a meal with the same folks she talked to and spent time with every day. But the way she was acting, you would think that the president was coming and bringing Nelson Mandela with him.

"Brook, Brook…hey Brook!" Tameka screamed.

"Yeah, what is it?"

"What is wrong with you, why are you running around here like a chicken with its head cut off?"

"In case you don't realize it, Christmas is in two days. Do you understand what that means? It means that the food has to be cooked, house has to be cleaned, gifts have to be wrapped and I only have two days."

"You need to calm your ass down. The house is clean already; the housekeeper was just here yesterday. The major food items are coming from Honey Baked Ham and if you don't take the time to finish one thing before you start another, you'll never get done with the rest of this crap."

"I guess you have a point."

"Take a break, let's have some tea and a little conversation and then together we can take care of whatever has to be done."

"I guess I can do that."

Tameka went in the kitchen and a few minutes later came out with hot tea and cookies for Brook and hot chocolate for herself. They sat down around the coffee table in the family room and settled into conversation.

"So, tell me why you're really so jumpy about this Christmas dinner?"

"Because I've invited someone else to join us."

"Oh, now I see. Would this someone else happen to be Eric?"

"Yes, it is Eric and he's bringing a friend with him, a guy named David. He's new to town and I told Eric to bring him along so he wouldn't be all by himself."

"Is he cute?" Tameka asked as she seemed to get excited.

"I hope so; I'd really love to hook him and Mia up."

"Why, Mia?"

"Because she could use a good man in her life and you already have Wayne. Remember him, your lover man?"

"Yeah, but there is always room for a new man, especially if he's a money man."

"Your priorities are all out of whack."

"Well Brook, that's easy for you to say. You'll never have to worry about money as long as you live."

"Money isn't everything, Tameka. Do you realize how strongly you could come to love someone that you've struggled with in order to build a good life together? A lot of time the money comes later if you stick with a good man. And then you'll actually appreciate it more than if it were just handed to you on a silver platter."

"It's real easy to say that when you're a multi-millionaire ain't it, Brook?"

"You just don't get it."

"No, you're the one who doesn't get it and you never will. If I end up with the wrong man, I could have financial struggles that you'll never know."

"Tameka, you act like you're poor now. In case you've forgotten you have a great career with CNN making excellent money. If you make a couple of wise investments and put some away, you'll never have to worry about money either. But more importantly, you need to understand that money isn't everything. I promise it can't keep you warm at night."

"Yeah, but a man with plenty of money can truly keep me warm."

"And what if he turns out to be the ugliest thing you've ever seem, but he's rich as cream, then what, Tameka?"

"Then I'll close my eyes, screw his brains out and wait to get paid."

"You are really sick. You would build a relationship with a man you can't stand to look at just so you can get your hands on his money. You need therapy."

"You need to watch your mouth. Don't pass judgment on me when you haven't walked an inch in my shoes."

"And I never want to be in your shoes because with that mentality, you and your shoes are going to hell with gasoline pants on."

"Fuck you, Brook!"

Tameka looked at Brook as if she wanted to kill her, but instead she jumped up, grabbed her purse and her coat and headed for the door.

"Tameka, please don't leave. I wasn't trying to pass judgment. I was really just kidding with you. Tameka…" The next thing Brook heard was the door slam and she immediately regretted the entire conversation.

Brook got up from the couch, placed their dishes on a tray

and headed for the kitchen. She finished cleaning the kitchen, moved on to the family room and made sure it and every other room was clean. She sat down and reviewed the dinner menu. The ham and turkey were coming from Honey Baked, along with all of the desserts. She would get up first thing in the morning to cook, chop and mix everything for the dressing, green beans, yams, collard greens and cranberry sauce. Brook picked up the phone to call Mia, but remembered that she was at church for her women's group Christmas celebration. Brook hung up the phone and headed for her bedroom. She went to her closet and pulled out all of her wrapping paper, ribbon, bows and tape and carried it all to her bed. She then went back to the closet, reached in the very back and started pulling out gifts. Brook settled on her bed and began to wrap presents. This was a task that usually filled her with a joyful spirit, but tonight she couldn't find that joy, it was hiding behind the grief she felt about making Tameka feel so badly. Brook stayed up until 1:15am hoping to talk to Tameka, but she never returned home. Brook thought about calling over to Wayne's house, but remembered he was out of town for the holidays. Tameka must have been at her mothers and it was much too late to call over there. Brook rolled over in her bed and went to sleep.

Tameka finally returned home at 10:30am Christmas Eve morning, she went straight to her room and closed the door. Brook waited as long as she could for Tameka to come out before she jumped up and went to Tameka's room and knocked on the door. There was no answer, she knocked again.

"Tameka, please open the door and talk to me? Please?" The door swung open and Brook entered the room. "I am so sorry, I never meant to put you down or make you feel badly. I really was just kidding; I love you and think that you're such a smart and accomplished woman. I didn't mean to hurt you." Brook spoke as tears rolled down her face. After standing for a few seconds without any response from Tameka, Brook turned to walk away.

"Brook, it's okay. Let's just forget it. Give me a few minutes to take a shower and throw something on and I'll come in and help you with tomorrow's dinner."

Brook turned around and gave Tameka a huge hug.

Both Brook and Tameka worked tirelessly to finish dinner. They only stopped long enough to run and pick up the turkey and other major food items and grab a little lunch. They both felt a sense of accomplishment and pride with all that they had done. Mia was coming over tonight for the three of them to have a little private celebration and gift exchange. Brook had managed to get both Mia and Tameka to promise to play nice and make this a drama free evening and Christmas day. Brook headed to her room to shower and dress for the evening as did Tameka. At 8:00 pm Mia was at the door with an arm full of gifts and food for the night.

"To the three of us, may this be a holiday filled with love, fellowship and friendship." Mia and Tameka lifted their glasses to join Brook in her toast.

"That was beautiful, now let's eat. What all did you bring, Mia?" Tameka asked.

"Girl, we've got wings, potato salad, rolls, chips, dip and deviled eggs. I decided to keep it kind of light since we'll be eating so heavy tomorrow."

The three of them sat down and ate until their hearts were content. This was turning out to be a better night than Brook had anticipated. She couldn't believe that Mia and Tameka were getting along so well, actually acting like old friends. This had to be her Christmas miracle. After cleaning up their dishes and putting the remaining food away, they all headed for the Christmas tree and sat around it like anxious little children.

Tameka grabbed two boxes and handed one each to Brook and Mia. "Brook, thank you for being such a wonderful friend and sharing your home and life with me. Mia, I hope that this will be a building block for us, the beginning of a real friendship."

Brook opened her gift and there was a beautiful 24k gold charm bracelet with a heart dangling from it and her mom's name engraved on one side and her father's on the other. Brook was speechless; she never knew that Tameka could be so sentimental. Brook reached for Tameka and gave her a kiss on the cheek and a strong hug, she was truly touched. Mia opened her box and found a gorgeous pink Baby Phat sweater. She couldn't believe that Tameka actually got her something so nice.

"Tameka, this is so beautiful, thank you so much. I hope that this can be a new beginning for us."

Mia then handed out her gifts and anxiously waited for them to be opened. Tameka ripped the paper off of the light weight box and found a gift certificate for a day of pampering from Spa Sydell. "Thank you Mia, this is fabulous. I can't wait to use it."

Brook opened her gift and found the same thing that Tameka had received. "Okay ya'll,

before you think I've lost my mind for getting you the same gift let me explain. I thought it would be so much fun for us all to enjoy a spa day together." Brook reached over and hugged Mia.

"Thank you Mia, I think that this is such a cool gift. We get to be pampered and spend such a relaxing day together. This is really thoughtful."

Brook then passed out her gifts to her friends. Mia opened her box and there was the beautiful Jones New York suit she had been admiring. She screamed like a little girl, grabbed Brook and planted a big kiss on her cheek. "Thank you, thank you, thank you!"

Seeing what Mia had gotten, Tameka couldn't wait to open her present. Tameka tore the

box open and found a pair of Dolce & Gabbana boots she had wanted but refused to buy for herself. "Brook, I don't know how to thank you. I love you man, you're the bomb, you're my girl. As far as gifts go, this is the best Christmas I've ever had. Thank you guys so much."

The three friends sat around for a couple more hours talking and drinking wine. Once the wine bottle was empty, they decided to call it a night. Mia had brought her clothes over so that she could spend the night and be fresh for Christmas day. Tameka went to bed first and as Mia headed for the guest room Brook stopped her and suggested that she sleep with her instead of the guest room. Without hesitation Mia agreed and they retired to Brook's room.

"I know you think I'm silly for wanting you to sleep with me, but I just really wanted to talk for a while."

"Well, Brook, I'm all about conversation. Was there something specific you wanted to talk about?"

"I wanted to get your opinion on a little falling out me and Tameka had yesterday. I upset her so badly and I didn't mean to. I was honestly just kidding around. Maybe I really did mean some of what I said but I didn't mean to hurt her."

Brook went on to tell Mia the details of the conversation and wanted to know her take on the entire situation.

"I don't think that there is a need for you to feel bad. You simply said how you felt and I probably would have said some of the same things. It would be hard not to react to the type of comments she made, I mean she's obviously a gold digger."

"I don't know that she's a gold digger at all. Maybe she just thinks that a financially set man is the only way to ensure that she never has to go back to a life of poverty."

"Maybe, but Tameka makes a darn good living on her own. She could support herself in a very comfortable way. Don't get me wrong, I'm glad that me and Tameka are truly going to work on a friendship, but don't let the goodness of tonight blind you to the type of person we know her to be."

"Mia, sometimes I just think that we don't understand her and maybe judge her a little too harshly."

"Brook, I didn't grow up rich. I grew up in a middle class family that had to work hard to get what we wanted. My parents struggled just like Tameka's mom did and I realize that we still had it better than them, but my point is that Tameka isn't the only one who's known struggles. A hard or deprived up bringing doesn't give you the right to treat people badly or use folks to get ahead and that's what Tameka does."

"I know, but maybe if we were just more patient with her and talked to her more about her own abilities, she wouldn't have that mentality."

"Girl please! Tameka is not a child, she is what she is and that's a woman who uses other people for her own selfish purposes. We can't mold her and I don't even want to try. You are going to have to accept what is and handle her appropriately."

"I know that what you say is true, but I hate writing her off as no more than a selfish gold digger when I know she's capable of so much more."

Brook and Mia never realized that Tameka was standing outside of the bedroom door for the better part of their conversation. She heard just about everything and couldn't believe the nerve of these stuck up bitches. Who the hell did they think they were? They really thought that they were just so superior to her morally and ethically. She felt that they talked about her as if she were the gum on the bottom of their shoes and after she spent her hard earned money on them. Well, if they wanted to think so little of her, she decided that she'd give them reason to do so. It was time to kick up her game and let them see just how morally bankrupt she could be.

# CHAPTER FOURTEEN

Ms. Williams was the first guest to arrive for the Christmas day celebration. She had been so anxious to see where her daughter was now living and couldn't believe that Tameka made her wait so long. But once she stepped through the door she forgot about all of that and was completely in awe of her surroundings. Brook greeted her with a big hug and volunteered to give her a little tour of the place. She first saw the dining area that housed the most exquisite china cabinet and dinner table she'd ever seen. The table setting was just like something she'd seen in a magazine, all of that crystal and silver. They moved on to the family room and Ms. Williams couldn't believe that they actually made ceilings that high for private residences. The furniture was beautiful and she just loved that chaise lounge and flat screen plasma television up on the wall. When they entered the kitchen Ms. Williams thought she'd died and gone to heaven. The maple cabinets, island with the built in grill, ceramic flooring, double ovens and smooth stovetop were more than she could have ever imagined.

"Child I could cook in here every minute of every day." They all chuckled and moved on to the bedrooms. The guest room was very basic with a four poster bed, dresser with mirror and chest of drawers. It was the bedding and floral arrangements that made it stand out. Tameka's room had a lovely knotty pine queen size bed, dresser and mirror and entertainment center. Brook's bedroom was very large with a gorgeous cherry wood king sized sleigh bed. It was complete with dresser and mirror, armoire and a large sitting area that held a love seat, coffee table and built in book shelves. Ms. Williams especially loved the fire place that was built into the wall between the bed and bathrooms. She never knew anyone who actually lived this well.

"Brook, your home is so beautiful. I have never seen anything like this before in my life, well except for those magazines. And it was just so nice of you to let Tameka live with you."

"Well Mama, it's not like I live here for free."

"I know baby, but it's still nice of Brook to open up her home to you. Not everyone would do that."

"Yeah, Ma, whatever."

"It's not nice to use that tone with your mother Tameka." Ms. Williams stated matter-of-factly.

"I didn't mean anything by it Mama, but you act like I'm some poor orphan that Brook took in. I pay my own way; no one is giving me a hand out."

"You know what, baby; I didn't mean to start an argument. Ya'll have obviously worked hard to make this a nice day so let's just really try and enjoy it."

"I couldn't agree more, Ms. Williams. Let's all go into the kitchen and I'll fix us some drinks," Brook stated in an effort to try and create a light, festive atmosphere.

Within the hour Eric and his friend David had arrived. They all sat around for a while sipping wine and getting acquainted with one another. David seemed to be a really nice guy that was quit interested in Mia. Tameka tried to gain his interest but he wasn't taking the bait. Mia and Brook kept looking at each other as if to say *what the hell is she doing?* Tameka's behavior was so out of line. She was strutting around in a skin tight sweater, ultra mini skirt and three inch heels bending over every chance she got. As they prepared to go into the dining room for dinner, Ms. Williams pulled Tameka over to the side.

"Tameka, what in the world is wrong with you? You're strutting around like a two bit whore working a street corner. I know I raised you better than this. These men are taken, so stop trying to get their attention and remember that you already have a man. Remember Wayne?"

Without a word Tameka snatched her arm away from her mother's clutch and walked away. She walked right into the dining room and grabbed the seat right beside David before Mia could sit down. Everyone was shocked, but without saying a word, David rose from his seat, pulled a chair out for Mia and sat on the other side of her. Tameka had not planned to have to look over Mia just to get a glimpse of David. Once everyone was seated, Brook asked Eric to lead them in prayer and then they all enjoyed a meal fit for a king.

Once everyone had finished dinner, Brook fixed hot tea and coffee for everyone to enjoy in the family room. She then started clearing the dishes and was surprised when Eric walked up beside her and started helping her clear the table.

"You don't have to help me with this, you're a guest. You should be in there relaxing."

"Being with you relaxes me. Besides, the faster we clear the table, the faster you can join the rest of us."

Brook smiled as she continued to clean the dining room. She and Eric were done in no time and then went to join everyone else. She was not pleased, but no longer surprised to see Tameka still trying to get her hooks in David. They all sat around talking for another fifteen minutes when Ms. Williams asked Tameka to please take her home. Tameka was extremely annoyed and actually had the nerve to ask her mother how she'd gotten there. When Ms. Williams answered, "I took a taxi," Tameka angrily stood up, got her coat and keys and headed for the door.

"Ms. Williams, I'm so glad you joined us today and before I

forget, I got you a little something for Christmas. Wait one second, I'll be right back." Brook went to the tree and retrieved the gift.

"Oh baby, you didn't have to do this. You've already done so much, welcomed me into your home and shared your holiday with me. I didn't even get you a thing."

"Ms. Williams, your being here was the best present you could have given me."

"Thank you baby, and I'm sorry about Tameka's behavior, I don't know what's gotten into her."

"Don't you worry about her. Would you like to take a plate home?"

"Brook, I'm so full that I wouldn't even be able to eat it. Besides, I cooked a small hen and some sides just in case my son stops by later."

"Well okay, thank you again for coming." They shared a warm hug and Ms. Williams left to catch up with Tameka.

Brook returned to the family room and turned on a little jazz music. "Is this okay with everyone? I just always assume that everybody likes jazz."

"It sounds great to me" Eric stated.

There was no response from Mia or David, they were so into one another and their conversation that they didn't even hear Brook's question. Brook looked at Eric and smiled while pointing at their friends. She then joined Eric on the sofa and was a little shocked when Eric asked her if she had a big blanket.

"Yes…why?"

"I would love to snuggle with you, purely innocent, out on the terrace."

"Eric, do you know how cold it is outside?"

"Of course, that's why we need the blanket." Eric stated with a smile. "I promise I'll behave myself."

"You better behave, let me get the blanket and I'll meet you outside Mr. Banks."

Brook disappeared around the corner while Eric grabbed a

bottle of wine and two glasses. She felt so safe as she and Eric snuggled on the lounge chair under the stars. They shared excellent conversation and spine tingling kisses. After two hours they heard a knock on the terrace door and then it opened. Mia appeared beside them.

"Well, don't you two look cozy?"

"We are, you should try relaxing out here some time," Brook replied.

"Thanks, but no, I prefer the warmth of the indoors. I came out to let you know that David and I both have early mornings and are about to leave."

They all went back inside where Eric advised Brook that he'd have to leave as well since David rode with him.

"No man, don't worry about it, don't let me rain on your parade. Mia has been kind enough to offer me a ride." David stated with a mischievous grin.

"You sure you don't mind?" Eric asked Mia.

"Not at all, Mr. Walker's home is actually not that far from mine," Mia replied with a smile.

Brook retrieved Mia and David's coats and they all said their goodbyes. But deep down inside Brook was glad they were gone and that Eric was still there with her.

"You know Brook, I'm really glad we're alone now. I have something for you but I'm so shy I didn't want to hand it over in front of everyone."

"Yeah right, you're shy," Brook stated sarcastically.

Eric went and took something out of his coat pocket and returned to Brook with a more serious expression.

"I wanted to get you something as a token of my appreciation. I appreciate your beauty. I appreciate your strength and I appreciate your letting me into your life."

"But I didn't get you anything."

"Trust me Brook; you've given me a hell of a lot," Eric stated. He handed Brook a small jewelry box. Brook opened it and found a gorgeous diamond and opal pendent hanging from a gold necklace.

"Eric, this is so beautiful, I don't know what to say…thank you."

"You are more than welcome," He said as he placed it around her neck.

They stood face to face and Eric leaned in to kiss Brook. She wrapped her arms around him and for the first time, in a long time, Brook let go and allowed herself to be loved, completely loved.

# CHAPTER FIFTEEN

Brook had never been so happy to be at work, she was happy to be anywhere. Brook was just happy to be alive. She hadn't felt this kind of joy since her parents were alive. She felt a little guilty for being this happy without them and prayed that they would understand. Brook knew that her mom and dad would want her to be happy and felt that they would have approved of Eric; he was such a good man.

"Penny for your thoughts."

"Huh?" Brook replied to Mia's comment. "What did you say?"

"I said penny for your thoughts girl. Where is your head right now 'cause it sure isn't on this job today."

"What time is it?" Brook asked.

"11:15, why?" Mia asked with a puzzled look on her face.

"Let's go to lunch, my mind really isn't on my work and maybe a little break would help."

"Give me a few minutes; I'll meet you out front at 11:30, okay?"

"Alright."

Mia and Brook sat at a small table in LaPatite café waiting for their brunch to be set on the table. The waitress came to the table with their water and coffee. Mia just sat and looked at Brook for a while, wondering if she would snap out of her trance long enough to share a thought or two.

"Okay Brook, what is up with you? You're sitting around with this silly grin on your face and acting like a space cadet. Is there something you haven't told me because a necklace can only make a person so happy? After a while it wears off."

"Well, there may be one thing I didn't tell you." Brook took a long pause.

"I'm waiting Brook."

"We made love Christmas night after he gave me the necklace."

"You what?"

"Calm down Mia and lower your voice," Brook said with a snicker. "I know I told you I wasn't ready for all of that, but after such a great holiday and Eric making me feel so special and safe, I couldn't think of anything I wanted to do more."

Mia was still sitting with her mouth dropped open when the waitress returned with their food. Brook, on the other hand, picked up her knife and fork and dug right into her Belgian waffle, bacon and eggs.

"Mia, close your mouth and eat. Your food is going to get cold and trust me, a patty melt and fries are not good cold."

"So how was it?"

"Oh this is good, want to try the waffle?"

"Heffa, you know I didn't ask how your food is. How was the sex? And don't hold out on me."

"Mia, with him I felt like I truly could let go of all my inhibitions. I felt safe enough to completely let go and really get into it, really enjoy every aspect of it. I've never felt that way before. I've always felt like I had to hold something back, couldn't really let anyone see me completely lose control. But the things that man did to my body made me want to give him every part of me."

"Ooh girl, I'm happy for you and jealous as hell. I wish someone would make me lose control."

"Well, what about David?"

"Brook, he may just be the one to take me there but we need a little more time to get to know each other."

"But it does look promising?"

"Definitely!"

Brook raised her glass of water for a toast. "To us finding the love we deserve." Mia raised her glass and they tapped them together and drank a celebratory glass of water. The two women finished their lunch, paid the check and headed out the door. In the car ride back to work, Mia decided to ask about her new buddy Tameka.

"So, has she said anything about her behavior on Christmas day?"

"Child please, you know she didn't even come home for two days. I guess she spent some time at her mother's unless Wayne came back in town."

"I just can't figure out what got into her. Everything was going so good and then boom, she started acting crazy."

"Mia, you don't think she overheard us Christmas Eve do you?" Brook asked with a little bit of fear in her voice. The last thing she wanted was Tameka feeling like they were ganging up on her or attacking her character.

"I seriously doubt it, but even if she did, I don't see how throwing herself at David would make her feel better."

"Well, we're back at work now, so this has to go on the back burner. I've goofed off all morning and have to be productive for the remainder of this work day. We'll talk more about it later, okay?"

"Alright, see you later."

In an effort to make up for some of her earlier slacking, Brook didn't leave the office until 7:15 pm. By the time she got home, Tameka was already there fixing dinner.

"Something smells good, what is it?"

"I assumed you already ate, I only fixed enough for one."

"Oh, okay," Brook said with a puzzled look on her face. She hadn't seen Tameka in a couple of days and now she was greeted with such a cold attitude. Brook moved on to her room and placed her brief case down. She undressed, hung up her suit and put on old, comfortable sweats. Brook timidly made her way back to the kitchen, unsure of how to approach Tameka. She absolutely hated for tension to fill the air around her. She was always taught that home was the one place you could relax and feel free to be yourself. But tonight she was feeling like a stranger in her own home, it wasn't supposed to be this way.

"Tameka, are you having a bad day or are you having a problem with me specifically?"

"Brook, right now you are the least of my concerns. You need to stop being so damn arrogant, everything in this world isn't about you. You're not the little princess you think you are and I don't have to be all smiles just because I'm in your presence."

"Where is this coming from? Be honest with me, is there a problem between us that needs to be resolved? I never claimed to be anyone's princess, so I don't understand why you feel the need to talk to me like this."

"Oh, poor Brook. God forbid anyone talk to her in tones that aren't sugary sweet."

"You know what; I'm going out and get something to eat. Maybe that will give you a chance to calm down."

"Bye!"

Brook went and grabbed her purse, put on her shoes and coat and headed for the door. Brook had gotten down the hall when it hit her like a ton of bricks, "This is my damn house!" She exclaimed. Brook turned on her heels and headed back for the door. This was a situation that would be hammered out right here and now, but Brook refused to break and run from her own home. As she closed the door behind her, she could hear Tameka curse her return.

THE KNIFE IN MY BACK    83

"What's the problem?"

"I don't have a problem."

"Cute response, now try being honest. What's wrong?"

"Tell me Brook, why should I discuss anything with you when you choose to discuss things about us or more specifically me, with Mia? I heard ya'll the other night talking about me like I'm some gutter girl you're trying to lift to higher ground."

"Tameka, I'm sorry. To be honest, the talk me and you had kind of threw me. You are so strong, independent and self-suffi-cient, I don't get why you think you need to hook a man to live a good life. You should want to be with someone for love and companionship, not for a pay day. I shouldn't have talked about you behind your back, but the fact is you have been behaving like some hoochie gold digger. You have a good man, but still not satisfied with him. You require someone with more money, to hell with the kind of person he is. You were only interested in meeting David because you thought he may be a man of means and you had no shame in throwing yourself at him. Your mom was so embarrassed."

Without warning, Tameka snatched a knife from the butchers block and held the point of it to Brook's neck. "Bitch, you don't know shit about me or my mama." Tameka screamed the words at the top of her lungs. Then as quickly as she picked up the knife, she put it down and then broke down in mournful sobs. "Oh God, Brook I'm so sorry. I'm so sorry."

Brook was so thrown by that whole little scene. She just didn't know what to make of any of it. All she really knew was that she felt compelled to hold Tameka and tell her that it was alright. And that's just what she did. If only she could have seen the smirk on Tameka's face as she held her.

Still holding Tameka, Brook asked, "Tameka, why did you just do that?"

The only response she heard was sobs. Finally getting control of herself, Tameka replied "I don't know, I just lost my head. I'm so sorry."

"I completely understand, we all lose it at some time or another. However, I can't live with someone who may threaten my life at any given time." Brook could feel Tameka slowly pull away from her. "Tameka, you have until the end of the month to vacate my property and if you don't leave on your own, I will enforce our lease agreement and have you physically thrown out."

Tameka could not believe her ears. This had to be a joke. How could she have put herself in this situation? Before she could snap herself out of a state of disbelief, Brook turned and left the house. Tameka was now in a situation that she wasn't sure how she'd get out of. She loved this house and wasn't ready to give it up. There was absolutely no way that she would return to her mother's rat hole. This could not happen. No matter what she had to do, beg, cry or plead, she would not leave this house.

# CHAPTER SIXTEEN

---

Mia was so pleased with the direction she and David's relationship was heading. They had had several dates since they met Christmas day. Tonight they were sharing a meal at Dailey's and enjoying each other's company as they always did. Mia loved and appreciated how much of a gentleman David was. This was a quality missing in so many of today's men. Most men didn't understand that a strong, independent woman still enjoyed being treated like a delicate flower every now and then. But, David was perfect when it came to respecting her for her strength but still treating her like the lady she was.

"Mia, how is your work day looking tomorrow?"

"Pretty light, it shouldn't be bad at all. Why?"

"I was hoping I could talk you into playing hooky with me."

"I thought you had a client coming in tomorrow afternoon?"

"I can easily have another associate handle that for me. It's no big deal."

"Well, if you want me to play hooky it had better be for something darn good. Not just to sit around looking at soap operas."

"Well, how about I come over and prepare you breakfast? We can go and check out the new exhibit at the King Center and share a picnic lunch in the park. The rest we can just play by ear, what do you think?"

"I think that it's going to be a little too cold for a picnic, but I'd love to take you to lunch at this great little Thai restaurant."

"So that's a yes."

"Why not, I could use a day off. The holidays were a little hectic and a day of leisure would be a nice change of pace."

After dinner, Mia and David hung out at the piano bar for a while and then headed to Mia's home. Mia invited David in for coffee and conversation and that's just what they did. They talked for hours. The conversation flowed and both felt that they had never been able to share so much with any other person. Before they realized it, it was 2:40am. Unsure of what she was getting into, Mia extended an invitation for David to spend the night since it was so late. He accepted and they went to bed. Mia in her un-sexy pajamas and David in his t-shirt and pants laid down and fell asleep in one another's arms. It was the most intimate night of Mia's life. That night they shared more of themselves than could have been shared just by having sex.

# CHAPTER SEVENTEEN

When Tameka arrived at work, the office was all abuzz with talk about Craig. He had finally been tracked down…in a local hospital. Apparently, the police had contacted all of the news stations asking them to run a picture of some personal belongings of a man that had been found badly beaten in an effort to try and identify him. They couldn't actually show the man's face, but hoped that someone would recognize some of his personal items. When they presented the station manager with the photo of the belongings he couldn't believe what he saw. One of the items was a watch that the station sometimes presented to outstanding employees for years of exceptional work and dedication. The last person to receive one was Craig and he's the only one that hadn't reported for work in the last couple of weeks.

Monica came running up to Tameka the moment she saw her walk through the door. Tameka had always thought that maybe some of her co-works were suspicious about she and Craig's so called friendship.

"Good morning, Tameka, have you heard the latest about Craig?"

"No, Monica, but I'm sure you'll fill me in."

"Girl, he has been in the hospital for almost two weeks. The poor guy isn't even conscious. They say he's been beaten beyond recognition."

"Wow that is unbelievable. Do they know who did this to him?"

"No, they just figured out who he is. They are asking us to make this story our headliner and to give the police tip line number so that they can possibly get some leads."

"Well thanks for filling me in Monica."

"Are you going to see him? He's at Grady."

"Why would I go see him?"

"Well, I know that you all were close at one point. I'd still want to see my ex if he were hurt. You know, just to let him know I care about his wellbeing."

"Craig and I were associates, Monica, that's all."

"Yeah right."

"Think what you want, you small minded busy body."

"Ooh, touchy."

"Good-bye Monica."

Monica continued looking at Tameka as if she were willing Tameka to come clean about she and Craig's relationship.

"Good-bye Monica, you are dismissed. Get out of my face!"

Monica huffed off while Tameka got a cup of coffee and headed for her office. Before she started preparing for her work day, Tameka picked up her phone. She was relieved when her brother answered and told her that he'd primarily be hanging around the house all day. Tameka let him know that she'd be by to see him after work and that she fully expected him to be there.

Tameka left work a little early; she was more than a little anxious to speak with her brother. As she wheeled her car around through the city she found herself smiling an evil little smile. She could only imagine what was done to Craig and the worse the image the bigger Tameka's smile. She didn't really want to have anyone hurt, but reasoned that Craig more than deserved whatever he may have gotten. If he or anyone else didn't automatically treat her with the respect she deserved, she'd just have to demand it. Tameka would go to any lengths to be respected and get whatever she felt she deserved out of life. The only problem was that she felt she should have everything.

Tameka pulled up in front of a very rundown apartment complex. The city had vowed to refurbish these projects but so far they hadn't gotten around to it. She anxiously threw her car in park, jumped out and ran to the door. Before she could even knock, Derrick flung the door open and stepped outside.

"Hey, baby boy, why don't we go inside and talk?"

"My girls in there and she don't need to hear all my business"

"Well, you should think twice about being with someone you can't fully trust."

"Girl come on and let's just go sit in your car and talk."

They headed to the car and got comfortable inside. It was cold so Tameka started her car so that she could crank up the heat.

"We can't sit out here too long, gas is too damn high."

"Well then get to talking girl. You the one that came to see me."

"I just want to know what happened to Craig."

"Why do you care Tameka, you wanted him to suffer and he is. Can't that just be enough for you?"

"No damn it! Now tell me what you did. Please."

"Fine, Tameka. I followed him from work one day to see where he lived. A few days later I paid three crack heads to beat him down. They caught up with him in the back parking lot of his building. I gave them a little Polaroid camera so they could show me that they really did the job."

"You still got the pictures?"

"Are you crazy?"

"Okay, okay. That was a stupid question. How much did you have to pay them?"

"Girl I gave them motherfuckers a small bag of crack, no

more than four or five rocks. You should've seen them boys fighting over that stuff."

They both laughed at the idea of grown men fighting over little white rocks. While Derrick sold the stuff, neither he nor Tameka could understand how someone could be controlled by a drug. Both of them were too strong to give a none living thing that kind of power over their lives.

"Derrick, I really do appreciate you looking out for me and having my back."

"Hell girl, we all we got."

"Well thanks baby boy."

"No problem."

Derrick reached for the car door but before getting out; he leaned over and kissed his sister on the cheek. He then got out, closed the door and headed for his apartment. But just as he was about to walk out of sight, he heard Tameka call his name. He turned on his heels and stepped back to the car.

"What is it?"

"I just have one more favor baby boy."

"Aw hell Tameka, what is it?"

"Will you please give me a small glass vile with just one rock in it?"

"Tameka, I know damn well you better not be asking for this shit for yourself."

"Boy, are you crazy? You know I would never do anything like that to my body."

"Well why do you want it?"

"Let's just say that it's a gift for someone."

# CHAPTER EIGHTEEN

Brook and Eric were cuddled up in the lounge chair on her terrace with a nice thick blanket. They had enjoyed a day of rest and relaxation. Eric picked her up around 10:00 am and headed down Piedmont to the spa for his and her massages. After the spa they walked down the street to Wolfgang Puck's for a little lunch. They were supposed to go back to Brook's for a while and then meet up with Mia and David for a movie and dinner. But once they parked the car and got into the elevator those plans flew right out the window.

Eric found it impossible to keep his hands off Brook. As soon as the elevator doors closed, he pulled Brook into him and passionately kissed her. By the time the doors opened, Brook's legs were wrapped around Eric's waist and he was palming her butt. Luckily, no one was waiting for the elevator. They had only made love twice but Brook could tell that this time was different. As soon as they got inside, Eric was ripping Brook's clothes right off her body. He was very forceful with her and she loved it. She would never admit it to anyone but she loved the way that he was taking her. It was strong, manly and very sexy. Brook had never been so turned on. Eric had his way with her on the floor, her vanity, the shower and finally the bed. It was now time to cancel their evening plans and cuddle up.

"Brook, baby, the end of the month has come and gone and Tameka is still living here. Have you decided to just let her stay on in spite of what she did?"

"I don't know Eric. I can't help feeling sorry for her. I know that she never imagined she'd be living in a place like this and for me to force her out would be like breaking her heart into pieces."

"Well I'd rather have her heart broken than to have you dead. Just think about your safety."

"I am. I really don't think that she'd hurt me. That incident was kind of provoked by the fact that Mia and I had said such harsh things about her. She really felt that she'd been betrayed."

"I don't care what she felt, I simply don't trust her."

"I know, but I really think that she could improve for the better if she's just given a chance and feels that someone really gives a crap about her. She needs to feel respected and that she's on the same level with everyone else."

"That sounds like a mental issue to me, baby. One that requires the help of a professional therapist. Not one that you can improve by letting her get away with outrageous and dangerous behavior."

"Well, Eric, I'm not trying to cure her. I'm just trying to be a friend."

"Brook, you can't be everybody's friend. You can't be everyone's savior."

"I'm not trying to save… You know what, baby, let's just drop this conversation."

"Fine, we'll change the subject, but please be careful."

"Yes sir. Hey, my lunch is officially gone. Want to get some dinner? Maybe takeout."

"In a minute, right now I want you."

"A minute is all you need?'

"Smart ass."

Eric then flipped Brook onto her back and made love to her while the sun set on another beautiful day.

It was another work day. Brook rolled over when her alarm went off at 6:30am. She turned her radio on to V-103 so she could listen in on the Frank and Wanda Morning Show. She enjoyed hearing the entertainment news and lively, sometimes argumentative topics discussed by the morning crew. Brook pulled out one of her business suits, pumps and finally under-wear. She was feeling very sexy these days so she had gone to Victoria's Secret a couple of weeks ago and bought an entire new lingerie collection. Tameka thought it was wasteful and foolish for Brook to throw out all of the under garments she already had. Especially when some of it still had the tags on it.

After Brook showered and dressed, she went out to the kitchen for a little breakfast. Tameka was already sipping on a cup of coffee when she entered the room.

"Good morning. Is there any more coffee left in the pot?"

"Yeah, want me to pour you a cup?"

"Yes, please."

Brook moved around the kitchen, retrieving bagels, cream cheese and the toaster. She was thinking about what she and Eric had discussed the day before. While she didn't believe that Tameka would actually hurt her, she didn't want to put herself in a vulnerable position by being naive.

"Tameka, have you given any more thought to where you are going to move and when it might happen?"

"Well, I haven't found a place yet. I'm just torn as to whether I should buy or rent."

"Have you even been looking for a place, Tameka? Have you gone out even one day looking for a new house?'

"I've looked at a couple of apartment complexes, but I need a realtor to help me determine what type of house I should be looking at for purchase."

"No you don't, you know the type of place you want. No one else can make that decision for you."

"Brook, I just mean that I need someone to go through some listings with me."

"Do you want me to call Lauren for you?"

"No, we didn't have good chemistry. I'll find someone real soon."

"Tameka, you could always stay with your mom until you find something more permanent."

A look of sheer terror fell across Tameka's face. She looked as if her very life were being threatened.

"Brook, please don't force me into a corner where I'll have to go back there. I've told you how sorry I am and I swear nothing like that will ever happen again. I don't know what got into me, but I love you and would never hurt you. Please, just give me a little more time? Please?"

Brook finished her breakfast and gathered her things in preparation to leave for work. She knew that neither Eric nor Mia would be happy about what she prepared herself to say next.

"You've got one more month, Tameka and then you'll have to go. I don't care where, but you'll have to leave here."

Tameka grabbed Brook and gave her what seemed to be a sincere hug. Too bad Brook couldn't see her smirking behind her back. Tameka knew that she had Brook where she wanted her and that she could drag this moving thing out forever.

# CHAPTER NINETEEN

Tameka headed out to go see her mom. As she pulled out of the parking garage she took notice of the beautiful day. Despite the cold temperatures, the sun was shining and there wasn't a cloud in the sky. She was feeling good about her living situation and the fact that Craig had learned his lesson...or had he? Tameka wondered if he even realized why he had the hell beat out of him. She had heard that Craig finally woke up and after running a series of tests, the doctors determined that there was no permanent brain damage. Supposedly, he was healing well from a few broken bones and severe concussion. Maybe she would pay him a little visit after all.

Tameka pulled her car up in front of her mother's apartment and jumped out. When her mom opened the door, Tameka greeted her with a hug and kiss.

"Hey, Mommy."

"Hi, baby, come on in. Are you hungry?"

"No ma'am, I had a little breakfast not too long ago."

Tameka followed her mom into the kitchen where they shared a small pot of coffee and conversation. Ms. Williams was excited to show her daughter what she'd done to her old bedroom. Tameka always knew how much her mom loved to sew, so she wasn't the least bit surprised to see that her old room was now a sewing room. There was a mannequin in the corner with a partially sewn dress hanging on it. There was her old machine sitting on a table in the middle of the room. Ms. Williams had even gone out and splurged on a few small bundles of fabric.

"Mom, this is really nice. I'm glad you've got yourself something that you enjoy so much."

"And I do enjoy it, baby. This is the one thing I'm good at and it's so relaxing for me. My next goal is to save enough money so that I can buy myself an updated machine. The sewing machines they make now put my old one to shame."

"Are you going in to work today, Mom?"

"No, baby, I called in this morning. Everybody deserves a day to just take it easy and do what they want."

"I know the feeling. Hey, why don't you put your shoes on real fast and take a ride with me?"

"Well, where are we going?"

"It's a surprise, Ma, just come on."

The two women headed out and jumped into Tameka's car. As they made their way through the city, they enjoyed good conversation and the beauty of the day. They laughed and talked and Ms. Williams realized that she could still see the good and innocence in her baby girl. Tameka pulled the car into a parking space right in front of Joanne's. It was a huge sewing and crafts store. Tameka jumped out of the car and headed for the door before her mom could ask her first question. Ms. Williams hurried to catch up with her daughter and asked her what they were doing there.

"I need some things, Mom."

"Child please, we both know that you would never have a need for anything out of here," Ms. Williams said with a giggle.

"Hush your mouth old woman and come on," Tameka said as she laughed while grabbing her mom's hand and practically dragging her through the store. They stopped in the middle of the aisle with all of the sewing machines. As they started checking all of them out, a store clerk approached them. She took the time to show them each machine and explain the differences between all of them. She then had Ms. Williams sit down at several of the display machines and test them out. It was already obvious to Tameka which one she would purchase. Never mind that it was the most expensive one, her mom loved it and she loved her mom.

After the purchases were loaded into the car, the two women headed back to the apartment.

"Thank you so much, Tameka. That machine is some piece of work, it is gorgeous. And that sewing table you got for it to sit on is so beautiful. Thank you so much!"

Once they arrived at the apartment, Tameka paid a 19 year old neighbor to unload, assemble and set everything up for her mom. Tameka received an enormous amount of joy from watching her mom play with the machine and set up her sewing notions in all of the table drawers. She was truly like a kid at Christmas.

As a way of saying thanks Ms. Williams prepared lunch for her baby girl. Fried Tilapia, hush puppies and fries with plenty of hot sauce and catsup. Was it fattening, greasy and full of carbs? Of course, but it was good as hell. By the time Tameka finished eating, she had to unbutton her pants just to breath. Of all the fancy restaurants she had been to, Tameka couldn't remember a better meal. It was fabulously delicious.

"Baby girl, I can look at your plate and tell you enjoyed your food, but did you have enough?"

"Mama, I couldn't hold another bite. The food alone was worth missing a day of work."

"Speaking of work, Tameka, did you know the young man they found beat up a couple of weeks ago? They said he worked for your station."

"Yeah, I know him. He's one of the camera men."

"Well, why do you think someone would do something like that to him?"

"I don't know, Mama, maybe he crossed the wrong person. You know you have to

be careful how you treat folks these days."

"What makes you say that, was he a mean type person, do you know if he mistreated folks?"

"I don't know, Mama, I guess I was just fishing for an explanation."

They sat in silence for a little while longer looking at *The Young And The Restless*, Ms. Williams' favorite soap opera. Tameka sat there contemplating whether she should go and see Craig before he got released from the hospital. It didn't take her long to make up her mind. She hopped up, fixed her clothes and grabbed her hand bag.

"I'm going to be leaving now, Mama, do you need anything before I leave?"

"No, I think I'm in good shape. Where are you going?"

"Well, I think I'll run by the hospital to wish my co-worker a speedy recovery."

"Oh baby, that is so nice. I'm sure he'll appreciate it."

Tameka grinned a sly, evil little grin. She kissed her mom on the cheek and made her exit. Ms. Williams knew that there was something not quite right about that look she saw on her daughters face, but was afraid to ask or try to figure what it was all about. Sometimes she felt better off not knowing all that was going on with Tameka. Knowing everything could only put her in a position of doing the right thing and losing her child or keeping silent and always being afraid of what Tameka might do next. Sometimes ignorance really was bliss.

Tameka found a spot in the parking deck and made her way to the hospital entrance. After getting Craig's room number from the information desk, she stopped in the gift shop and purchased the cheapest bouquet of flowers they had and a pair of scissors. Tameka then took the elevator to the 5^th floor and headed for Craig's room. She was met in the hallway by a couple of other CNN employees that had just left their co-worker's sick room. They exchanged pleasantries and kept moving. Tameka stopped just inside of the door to Craig's room. He looked up and saw her standing there with a most unpleasant smirk on her face.

"What the hell are you doing here Tameka?"

"You mean after all of this you still haven't learned how to talk to people?"

"What do you want? Did you just come to rub salt in my wounds?"

"Oh, not a bad idea. Too bad I forgot my salt shaker. Seeing you in more pain would be such entertainment for me."

"Get out!"

"Shut up, Craig. What are you going to do if I don't leave, get up and kick my ass? I'd like to see you try. But speaking of kicking ass, looks like someone kicked yours pretty good. Did it hurt, did they catch you by surprise, what did they beat you with?"

"I'm glad to see you're finding joy in my misery...bitch."

"See, Craig, it's that kind of talk that landed you here in the first place."

Craig instantly sat up. "Did you have something to do with this; did you set me up to get beat like this?"

"Did I say that? I don't think that I did this. Besides, I don't hang out on your side of town."

"How do you know it happened on my side of town? That information hasn't been released. Tameka, if you had anything to do with this I will kill..."

Before he could finish his statement, Tameka slammed him back down on his bed and grabbed her scissors. She held them right over his penis.

"See big boy, it's that kind of talk that will get you permanently disfigured and I'm not talking about your face."

In one fatal snip, Tameka cut all of the flowers from their

stems and they fell over Craig's genitals. Tameka dropped every-thing else in her hands and let it all fall on Craig. She turned to leave but suddenly stopped and kissed him right on the lips. Craig used the little strength he had to push her away. Tameka just smiled and left the room.

# CHAPTER TWENTY

Brook was a little excited about her dinner date with Eric, Mia and David. She always enjoyed their little double dates. It made her completely happy to be around people she cared about and that cared about her. It had been a while since all of them had been out together and the fact that they were all going out on Valentine's Day was really special. The guys were taking them to dinner and then to a small dance club. After that, it was every couple for themselves.

Brook was putting the finishing touches on her make-up when she heard Tameka come through the front door. She continued what she was doing as Tameka entered her room.

"Ooh, look at you getting all dolled up. What's the occasion?"

"Hey, Tameka, have you forgotten? It's Valentine's Day!" Brook stated with a big grin on her face.

"And I see you're mighty excited about it. What are your plans?"

"Me and Eric are going out with Mia and David for a night of dinner and dancing. What about you?"

"Well I'm not going out with ya'll that's for sure. You could've at least invited me and Wayne to join you guys."

"I'm sorry Tameka, I honestly didn't even think about it. I guess I just didn't think that you would want to go."

"I'm just saying an invitation would have been nice. But that aside, me and Wayne are having dinner and after that, who knows. I guess we'll just play the evening by ear."

"Sounds good. Don't do anything I wouldn't."

The door bell rang and Tameka went to answer it.

"Hi, Eric, come on in. Brook should be ready in a second."

Tameka returned to Brook's room and let her know that Eric had arrived. Surprisingly, Tameka gave Brook a sweet, gentle hug and told her to have a great Valentine's. Brook returned the sentiment, gathered her things and left on her date.

Tameka went into her room to prepare for her own date. She skimmed her closet for a sexy outfit and finally settled on a little black dress. You could never go wrong with a LBD. She carefully laid out her under garments and headed for the shower. A half hour later Tameka felt refreshed and was looked great. She left for Wayne's house to get her own date started. As she headed across town, she thought of her mom and realized that she had no one special in her life on this day meant for lovers. With that in mind, she swung her car into Publix parking lot, went in and bought her mom a bouquet of flowers and a box of her favorite candy. It didn't take her long to drop it off and head out again for Wayne's house.

Eric held the door open for Brook as they stepped into Dailey's. It didn't take long to spot Mia and David across the room.

"Brook, girl you look fabulous." Mia stated with a broad smile and a warm hug.

"I'm just trying to keep up with you, super model."

They all shared in a little small talk until the hostess escorted them to their table. They enjoyed one another's company while feasting on the best food and most expensive wine that the restaurant had to offer. Neither Brook nor Mia had imagined their love lives would be this great and the men knew that they had each been blessed beyond their expectations.

Tameka walked in the front door that was being held open for her by someone that appeared to be a waiter. As she made her way into the family room, she saw Wayne standing by the fire place. The fire was crackling and the room twinkled with candle light. Wayne greeted her with a gentle kiss and a glass of champagne, Tameka was completely blown away by the atmosphere. The waiter appeared again and escorted Wayne and Tameka to the dining table that had been beautifully set with fine china and fragrant flowers. No one had ever done anything this sweet for Tameka; she was deeply touched by Wayne and his apparent love for her.

Brook crossed the threshold into Eric's home. They had completely enjoyed their evening out with friends but now they were ready for a little alone time. As soon as Eric removed Brook's coat he pulled her into his arms and kissed her with a passion that neither had ever known before. He then swept her up and carried her into his bedroom. Eric laid her on a bed covered with rose petals. As he turned on the fire place Brook realized that she was lying beside a cute little teddy bear.

"Aw, Eric, the bear is so sweet. I can't believe how thoughtful you are."

"Baby, I can't believe how blessed I am to have you in my life. You know that I love you, right?'

"Of course I do, I love you too, baby."

"Then if you love me, if you really love me the way that I love you, will you please marry me?"

Eric then held the teddy bear in front of him so that Brook could see the ring hanging from the ribbon around its neck. Brook grabbed the bear, not believing her eyes. She looked at Eric with tears falling down her face; she leaned in to kiss him and then softly said "yes". Eric removed the ring from the bear and placed the two and a half karat solitaire on Brook's finger.

Brook grabbed her man and kissed him deeply and they made love that night as if they'd never get the chance again.

Tameka kissed Wayne again as she rolled off of him and back onto the bed. She had never had a lover like Wayne before. A man that knew the art of making love. How to please her in every way and take control of her, but wasn't afraid to let himself be controlled and dominated from time to time. The man knew all too well how to please her and take her where no one ever had before.

"Tameka, baby, I've laid some towels out for us, why don't we jump in the Jacuzzi?"

"Sounds good, last one there gets spanked," Tameka said with a devilish grin.

Placed by the Jacuzzi were a couple of towels, a thick bath robe with a rose and a velvet box sitting on top of it. They stepped into the water and Tameka couldn't help but look back at the box.

"Tameka, you already know that I love you and would do anything for you. Now I would like for you to give me the opportunity to make you happy for the rest of your life. Will you please marry me?"

Wayne then opened the box and placed the one karat pear shaped diamond ring on Tameka's finger. "Yes, baby, I'll marry you. I will marry you." Tameka kissed her man and the love making started all over again.

# CHAPTER TWENTY-ONE

Tameka was bouncing off of the ceiling as she ran around the house getting herself ready for work. She kept on looking down at her ring finger and giggling like a school girl. She had never been so happy before in her life. Finally, her own little ray of sunshine, a spark of light that belonged to her and her alone. No one could take this joy. She was headed into the kitchen when she heard the door open and Brook enter the house. She started a pot of coffee and was soon joined by Brook.

"Good morning Brook. Aren't you keeping late hours these days? Last night must have been one hell of a Valentine's Day."

"Yes it was." Brook sang out.

"Damn, you're happy. I'm glad to see my friend so chipper. And if you can't tell, I'm pretty darn happy myself." Tameka said as she held up her hand to reveal her engagement ring.

"Oh my God Tameka, you're engaged? You and Wayne are getting married, that's wonderful." Brook screeched as she grabbed Tameka up into a tight embrace.

"Yes girl, I'm engaged. Isn't my ring gorgeous?"

"Tameka it is lovely. I am so happy for you. Have you told you're mom yet?"

"No, I haven't had the chance yet. I'm going to see her after work."

"You are so lucky that you get to share this with your mom. I wish my mom were here for me to share the news with."

"You'd want to share my engagement with your mom?"

"No, crazy," Brook said as she held up her hand to reveal her own sparkling diamond. "I got engaged last night too."

Tameka instantly felt Brook step into her sunshine. "You're engaged?"

"Yes, why do you sound so shocked? Aren't you happy for me?"

"Of course I am." Tameka responded very dryly.

"You sure don't sound like it."

"Forgive me, I truly am happy for you. I guess I had it in my head that this was my time to shine and be happy. My day in the sun. But hey, if I got to share it I'm glad I get to share it with you."

"This is both our time. I know how you feel but we can both shine along with the other 50 million people that got engaged on Valentine's Day." Brook said with a laugh.

"Yeah, you're right. I've got to get out of here, I'm already running late." Tameka grabbed her travel mug of coffee and headed out the door.

Brook knew in her heart that Tameka was still upset about having to share the spot light. Brook couldn't understand why Tameka felt this way, getting engaged on a particular day wasn't what made the engagement special. It was the man you were engaged to and the way in which he proposed. That should have been enough for Tameka.

Tameka was furious! She sped down the street angry that she couldn't have just this one moment to herself. She was pissed that Brook could have the nerve to find humor in her disappointment. Tameka didn't give a rat's ass if fifty million people got engaged last night. All that mattered to her was that she be the only one in her circle of friends and associates to get engaged at this particular time. And that bitches ring, it was huge. Why couldn't Tameka at least have the bigger diamond? It all just seemed very unfair to her.

Brook made her way into the office, still floating on air. She couldn't wait for lunch so that she could share all of her news with Mia. As she arrived at her desk, she was greeted by an enormous bouquet of flowers. Beautiful, exotic flowers. She'd never seen anything so amazing in her life. She grinned ear to ear as she read the card from her fiancé. As happy as she was, how could her employer really expect her to work. She was just too happy to concentrate on work, but she sat down to get started and do the best that she could.

At twelve noon Brook's phone rang and she was pleased to hear Mia on the other end saying that it was time to go to lunch. Brook didn't hesitate to sign off her computer, grab her purse and go. Just as the two women were about to approach one another, Brook turned and removed her ring, placed it in its box and gently placed the box in her purse.

"Come on, girl, what are you doing?"

"Stop yelling at me, I'm coming."

They hopped in the car and headed for Houston's. As they waited for their table to become available, Mia shared what she and David did after they left Brook and Eric the night before.

"Ooh, Brook, it was such a nice night. We took a carriage ride through town and then we took our time and walked back to the car hand in hand. David is so sweet and caring and gentle. I could really see myself with him long term."

"Look at little Miss Mia gushing all over the place about her man. Girl, you sound like you're in love."

"Let's just say that I feel myself falling. I'm trying to be careful though. Remember, we just met at Christmas, I don't want to move too fast."

"I don't know, Mia, sometimes you have to let go and free fall. Just remember to pray on your way down," Brook said with a smile.

"Yeah, well, I might not be able to stop myself from falling. He took me back to my place where he gave me this beautiful tennis bracelet and we shared a little intimate time," Mia stated as she held up her arm for Brook to see.

"This is gorgeous. Go, Mia, you got busy girl?"

"I didn't say that, I said we shared some intimate time and trust me, there are a lot of ways to be intimate without going all the way. I just don't think I'm ready to go there yet and David is extremely understanding about that."

"Well good for you. I want you to do whatever is going to make you happy and make you feel comfortable and sure of things."

As their food was placed in front of them, Brook slipped her ring back on her finger. Without saying a word she reached over her food for the salt shaker that was resting right in front of Mia. As she lifted it from the table her ring finger was the only one not gripping the salt shaker. Before she could move her hand back, Mia grabbed it and let out a loud squeal. Several people turned to look in their direction but they were now oblivious to everything and everyone around them.

"Oh my God, Brook, did Eric propose? Are you getting married? How did it happen? This is one freaking rock!"

"Slow down, Mia, I'll tell you everything."

As they ate and fussed over the ring, Brook shared everything about her special night. By the time she finished her story her face actually hurt from smiling so much.

"Now, here is the part you're not going to believe. Guess who else got engaged?"

"Who?" Mia asked with a puzzled look on her face.

"Tameka."

"Girl, stop playing."

"Mia, I am serious. She has a beautiful ring and was so excited."

"So Wayne popped the question."

"Yes, girl. She only lost her enthusiasm when I told her that

I'd also gotten engaged . That did not seem to set well with her. It seems she wanted that to be her special day."

"Does she realize how many people get engaged on Valentine's Day?"

"That's what I told her, but it meant nothing to her. Even after I told her that it's the way her man proposed to her that makes the day special, she didn't seem moved. Just annoyed."

"Humph, she'll be alright."

"Yeah, you're right. Ready to head back to work?"

## CHAPTER TWENTY-TWO

Tameka headed into the office with a smile on her face. She had found a way to put her negative feelings about Brook's engagement behind her. She glanced at her ring as she maneuvered her way through the building and couldn't help but be happy with the fact that she was loved by a good man. The only thing that could make it better would be if Wayne earned a higher salary. But she would worry about lighting a fire under his career and ambitions later. Right now she would just enjoy her day and the idea of planning a wedding. Then her thoughts were cut short as she was greeted by that annoying Monica.

"Good morning, Tameka. You look mighty happy today. Is there a reason"

"Hi, Monica, I didn't realize that I needed a reason to be happy."

"I guess I'm just not used to seeing you so chipper in the mornings."

"Well, my dear Monica, there is a first time for everything."

"Yes, there is a first time, but now I think I know why you're so happy. Is that an engagement ring on your finger?"

"You caught me, Monica, can't get a thing past you."

Without warning Monica let out a big squeal and grabbed

Tameka up into a bear hug. Of course this attracted damn near everyone's attention and people started to gather around asking what was going on. Monica made an announcement about the engagement as if she were the one getting married. Once the news room was all a buzz and everyone was gathered around, Monica had to throw a little hate Tameka's way.

"Hold your hand up higher, Tameka and let everyone see your precious little diamond. Isn't it a great starter ring everyone? It's just precious."

Tameka snatched her hand out of the air and it was apparent to everyone that she was pissed. How dare this little witch try and demean her and cut down her ring in front of everyone. And just when Tameka had decided to let her slide and not knock her out of the anchor chair. Well know the witch would pay. Monica had no idea how much this little stunt was going to cost her. As Tameka started to walk away she heard Monica call out behind her.

"Don't forget that we are doing lunch with Mr. Thomas today, Tameka."

Mr. Thomas was the station manager and he often got together with the anchors and producers to make sure that everything was going okay. Mr. Thomas prided himself on having happy, satisfied employees that weren't looking to go anywhere. Today he would have to decide whether to fire someone and their desire to stay or leave would not play into his decision at all.

Tameka threw herself into her work and made sure that Mr. Thomas and everyone else saw how well she performed. The noon day broadcast was flawless and while the audience would give all the credit to the anchor, folks that actually worked in the business knew how much credit went to the producer. But Tameka had once again decided that she wanted to shine to everyone. Not just industry people but to the average Joe on the street. After all, it was Oprah that everyone knew and not her producers. If Tameka could pull this off she would finally have recognition that Brook would never have.

"Tameka, great segment, you are really shinning around here. Outstanding job."

"Thank you, Mr. Thomas. I appreciate that."

"Are you ready for lunch?"

"Yes sir, just let me grab my purse and I'll be right back."

Tameka went to her office and as she gathered her things she saw Monica talking with Mr. Thomas. This was the perfect time to make her move. Tameka opened a locked drawer and picked up a small vile. She headed out of her office with a smile on her face and a spring in her step. "I'm ready," Tameka said, as she bumped into Monica, knocking her purse out of her hand. Monica's things spilled to the floor. And in the commotion, Tameka dropped the vile directly in front of Monica's purse.

"Oh Monica, I'm so sorry. Let me help you pick up your things."

"You should really watch where you're going, Tameka. A blind person could have seen me standing here."

"Goodness, Monica, it's okay, don't get so upset."

"Ladies, let me be the gentleman and pick them up," Mr. Thomas stated as he kneeled to retrieve Monica's belongings. He stopped short when he picked up the vile with a little white rocks inside. Mr. Thomas stood slowly and turned to Monica.

"Is this yours, Miss Greer?"

"Oh my goodness, Monica, is that why you've been acting so strange?" Tameka asked while shaking her head.

"I don't even know what that is. Where did it come from?" Monica asked defensively.

"Well, Miss Greer, it was at the opening of you bag. Looks like it fell out with the rest of your things."

"Mr. Thomas, I swear I don't know where it came from. It's not mine."

Mr. Thomas turned to Tameka. "Tameka, again that was a

great segment, but we're going to have to postpone lunch until another day. Miss Greer and I have some things to discuss."

"I completely understand."

Mr. Thomas ushered Monica off to his office with Monica continuing to rant and rave that the drugs were not hers. She didn't realize that her behavior was not helping her situation at all. Tameka headed off to lunch to celebrate this latest victory.

After having a field reporter fill in for a few days, Mr. Thomas agreed to give Tameka a shot as the noon day anchor. He specified that it was a trial run just to see how she did and how the public reacted to her, but Tameka knew that she could parlay this into a permanent position if she wanted to.

# CHAPTER TWENTY-THREE

David pulled his car into Mia's driveway. He looked in his rear view mirror to check himself and make sure he was as together as he felt he was. The nervousness he initially felt with Mia had now been replaced by his normal confidence and he was glad about it. David was never what one would consider to be a timid man when it came to women. Mia was just a little more than he was used to. She was a tall, statuesque woman that was far more beautiful than anyone else he'd ever dated. She was smart and self-sufficient. Mia didn't need a man for anything except companionship. So the man that stepped to her had better have his act together. Lucky for David, he did have all of his ducks in a row and wasn't easily intimidated. He was thrilled that he wasn't over powered by his nerves and that Mia had the chance to see the real David.

David stepped to the door and rang the bell. When he heard the lock turn he put a smile on his face, but as soon as the door opened, David's jaw dropped to the floor. Mia stood before him in a revealing little black lace chemise from Victoria's Secret and sling back pumps with the little fur ball on top. "Mr. Walker, are you going to come in or make me stand in the door way like this all night?" David slowly stepped into the house and looked around at all the candles and smelled the aroma of something delicious coming from the kitchen. He reached and pulled Mia into him and began to kiss her deeply.

Mia pulled away from his grip. "Tonight, you'll have to follow my lead. So be patient, sit back and relax."

David took a seat at the dining table as he was instructed and filled their glasses with the wine that was chilling in the ice bucket. He sat back and enjoyed his view of Mia going about the business of sitting a fine dinner on the table. He would definitely enjoy this date. David was not accustomed to women serving him in this fashion. It seemed that most women these days were looking to be wined and dined without having to do any more than be eye candy for the men. Unfortunately, there was an abundance of men willing to spend the money in hopes of getting a little something - something in return. In so many ways dating had become a game of pick your whore. So many women were willing to put out if a brother was willing to spend enough on them.

But Mia, she was a real woman. She valued herself and demanded a high level of respect just by the way she carried herself. David felt that this was the way all women should be and they would get so much more out of life than they were now willing to settle for. After all, wasn't real love and commitment more valuable than an expensive dinner or new pair of shoes?

Mia finished placing the food on the table and sat before David all prepared to eat. How in the world was he expected to sit patiently, eat and carry on conversation with her looking like that?

"David, I hope you don't mind my changing our plans. I know that you were looking forward to seeing that movie."

"Sweetheart, that movie is not going anywhere. I'd much rather be right here with you. By the way, you look amazing!"

"Thank you, I'm glad you like what you see. Please pass me your plate." David did as he was told and watched in awe as Mia placed food on his plate.

"So, babe, how was your day?"

"It was just okay until you opened the door. Then it took an awesome turn for the better."

"Oh please, David, you've seen me almost every day for the past three and a half months. What makes tonight so special?" Mia quizzed with a sly grin on her face.

"Let's just say that I've never seen quite this much of you. However, I'd love to see this much and more a lot more often."

"Well, let's just see what tonight brings and maybe then you'll be asking for something else a lot more often."

"Alright now, mama."

They both laughed and continued to enjoy their dinner of herb crusted chicken, garlic mashed potatoes and asparagus tips. As usual, the conversation was just as good as the meal. They were always happy to be in one another's presence. After dinner Mia moved as if she were going to clear the table. But once she stepped to David's side of the table she couldn't contain herself any more. She slowly straddled him and sat in his lap so that they were face to face. Before he could speak a word, Mia kissed David very deeply and very passionately. He placed his arms around her and pulled her into him even more. David was so strong and he had a grip on Mia that wouldn't allow her to escape his grasp. Mia moved from his mouth and began to kiss his neck and chest, she could feel his heart racing and his power growing between her legs. This excited her more than she realized it possibly could. She felt her own nipples harden underneath her chemise and moisture starting to dampen her thong.

"David, you've been so patient, but I want you so bad right now," Mia moaned.

"Mia, I would wait for you forever. I just want you to be sure. I don't want you to have any regrets."

"I won't, I will not regret this. I want you so badly…make love to me, David."

Without another word, David stood with Mia's legs still wrapped around his waist. He carried her into the bedroom and laid her on the bed of rose petals. It seemed that in one smooth motion David's clothes were off and Mia's sexy little gown was all gathered around her waist. It was Mia's plan to be in complete control of this night but she had to admit that with her inexperience, she'd only screw up her attempt at seduction.

"Mia, baby, tell me what you like, what do you want me to do to you?"

"Everything, David, do everything to me."

David kissed Mia passionately as he firmly stroked her breast. Mia's breath began to quicken as he moved down and took her nipple into his mouth. He slowly moved from one breast to the other and delighted himself in her moans. He took his time as he moved further down and then stopped once his mouth found her moisture. It was almost more than Mia could take. No one had ever done these things to her body before and she was loving every second of it. David took his time and loved Mia over and over that night, in every way that he knew how. And if he didn't know before, he knew now that he was in love. He knew how to make love to a woman but had never gone to such lengths to make sure that they were as pleased as Mia was. He wanted to satisfy her in every way, in and out of bed.

The next morning Mia was awakened by the smell of coffee brewing. She got out of bed and headed towards the kitchen.

"Good morning, princess."

"Good morning. What's going on here?"

"I thought I'd prepare a little breakfast for the sweetest woman in the world."

"Oh, David, you are so darn thoughtful."

"I'd prefer to be characterized as strong, manly, or something along those lines."

"Well, you're all of that too, baby."

"So what are your plans for today, Mia?"

"I don't really have any. I generally like to just play my Saturdays by ear."

"Well, how about hanging out with me for a little bit?"

David sat their plates on the table and they began to enjoy a meal of waffles and bacon.

"What did you have in mind?"

"Well, Mia, how do you feel about looking at some engagement rings?"

"Yeah right, David, I see you got jokes this morning."

"Baby, I'm serious. I love you. Wouldn't you like to at least think about marriage?"

"David, I think that the idea of marriage is really beautiful, but I don't think that we are at all ready. Marriage is such a huge step and it's not something that I want to rush. I only want to be married once and I want it to be forever."

"I hear you, babe, but let me ask, how long do you think you'll have to be with a person before you'll consider marriage?"

"I don't know, David. I just feel like we still have so much more to learn about one another. This is still a relatively new relationship. We are so young, the world is our oyster. Let's just take more time to enjoy where we are right now."

"I hear you, sweetie. Well, how about a matinee?"

"Now that I can do. We still haven't seen that movie with Terence Howard."

David and Mia finished their breakfast and went back to bed. Their afternoon plans changed once the kissing began.

# CHAPTER TWENTY-FOUR

Ms. Williams was in her sewing room working on her latest creation when she heard someone enter the apartment. She sprang to her feet and grabbed her baseball bat from the corner. Tameka managed to duck just in time. She almost caught a face full of wood.

"Mama, what the hell are you doing, trying to kill me?"

"Oh, baby, I am so sorry. I didn't know that you were coming by today. I thought you were one of these little crack heads running around here or something."

"I thought I told you to get yourself an alarm system installed, Mama. Then you wouldn't have to worry about someone walking in on you."

"All those things do is make a lot of noise. They don't stop anyone from busting in."

"Mama, that noise scares people away and alerts the police, fire and ambulance in case of an emergency."

"Well, that all sounds good but we both know that I can't afford another bill."

"I told you that I would pay for it. Besides, Mama, if you would just go on disability like I told you, you would get more money from the state than you earn on that little job."

"But, Tameka, look at me, there is nothing wrong with me."

"But I got a shrink who'll say that you are as unstable as a box of rocks. Then you can get disability and your social security."

"That is so wrong in every sense of the word. You have got to learn to stop being so morally corrupt."

"Well, Mama, sometimes that's the only way to get what you want out of life. You have to do what you have to do in order to get what you want."

"How sad that you really feel that way. I'm sorry that I somehow failed you, made you develop this warped way of thinking."

"You didn't fail me, Mama; I just refuse to settle for the life that you've had."

"First of all, my life has not been a bad life, God has been good to me. I promise you that things could have been a whole lot worse. Things were difficult at times, but there ain't a person in this world that don't get a little rain in their life. If you think that you are somehow exempt, then you are sadly mistaken."

Tameka stood before her mother and applauded. "Oh, Mommy Dearest, that was some speech, I'm so moved. All because of those words you just spoke I'm going to completely turn my evil little life around."

"What the hell did you come over here for Tameka? What did you want?"

"Mama, I just came to say hi and see what you think of my new position at work. Have you caught the noon day news report yet?"

"Yes I have and I think that you are doing a fine job. The camera loves you, baby."

"That's just what the station manager said. Apparently, the public loves me too. I've been offered the anchor position permanently if I want it. I'll even get a nice little boost in salary if I take the position."

"That's great but I thought you liked being a producer?"

"I do, Mama, but I do enjoy all the attention that I get from being out front. Besides, when it comes to the money it's the popular anchors that get paid. Look at Oprah, she's the one with the billions, not her producers."

"I see. Just remember that money isn't everything. By the way, what happened to that Monica Greer girl? I liked her."

"Better than me, Mama, did you like her better than me?"

"Get a grip, Tameka, I just said that I liked the child! I swear sometimes that it's you who needs to be out on mental disability."

Without another word Tameka grabbed her purse and headed for the door. Before she could make her great escape her mom asked a question that completely threw her.

"Tameka, are you the reason that Monica is no longer the anchor, did you have anything to do with it?"

Tameka swung the door open and left without saying a word. Her silence spoke volumes to her mother.

# CHAPTER TWENTY-FIVE

Mia sat in the beautifully embroidered chair that was to the right of a small podium surrounded by mirrors. She had walked the entire store twice as she waited for Brook to step out and model a new gown for her. She felt ambitious when she got dressed this morning and put on a pair of 3 inch heels with her jeans. This was a decision that Mia now regretted and she was very grateful for the chair she was now resting in. When Mia agreed to go look at wedding gowns with Brook, she thought that the experience might leave her regretting her decision not to accept David's proposal. But instead, it confirmed her answer of "it's too soon." The gowns were gorgeous and Brook's ring was enough to take your breath away. But Mia realized that once the wedding day was over you had to be prepared to live with that new spouse for the rest of your life. And while she did love David, Mia wanted there to be no questions or doubts on either of their part as to whether they would make it.

"Hello, Mia. Earth to Mia."

Mia looked up to see an angel in ivory.

"Brook…you look amazing! I can't believe how beautiful you are. That gown is perfect for you."

"You really think so?"

"Girl please, you know it's the best you've tried on so far."

"It is gorgeous isn't it! It's a Vera Wang, designer to the stars."

"This is the one Brook. You won't find anything better suited for you."

"I don't think so either, girl. I just thought that it would take me a heck of a lot longer to find one. This is only the second time I've been out looking."

"Well, Miss Mansfield, our shop does carry only the best and if we don't have it, we can order it." The sales associate interjected as she continued to carefully place pins in the gown.

"Ma'am, how long will it take for you all to complete the alterations?"

"Miss Mansfield, our seamstress can have the initial alterations completed within the week and then you'll just have to come in for one final fitting right before the big day."

"That sounds great; I'll definitely take this one. It feels like it was created just for me."

"Just like your man, Brook, created just for you," Mia said with a chuckle.

Brook returned to her dressing room and changed out of the gown. She stepped back out into the boutique with a grin on her face and her check book in hand. She grabbed Mia by the hand and headed to the front counter.

"Mia, I'm so happy that I am going to buy you lunch today. You pick the place and make it good."

"Ooh, my lucky day. How about Justin's?"

"You got it."

The sales associate appeared with Brook's gown and hung it behind the counter. "Miss Mansfield, is this your final choice?"

"Definitely, go right ahead with the alterations."

"You are aware that we don't have payment plans available and we require seventy-five percent down."

"No, I was not aware, but it's not information that I needed. I am quite capable of paying for this dress."

"I'm sorry, Miss Mansfield, I didn't mean to offend you. The gown is on sale for $25,500.00, seventy-five percent down will be $19,125.00 with the balance due upon delivery."

"Do you all accept personal checks?"

"Yes ma'am."

Brook wrote the check and took her receipt. She and Mia walked out of the door and headed for the car. Brook wanted to be angry about the exchange of words between her and the sales person, but she was just too excited about her purchase. So instead of being upset, she shook off that bad vibe and looked at Mia with a wide toothed grin.

"I refuse to let that heffa steal my joy."

"That's right girl, it's all about you today and you have too much to be happy about."

Brook and Mia headed on through down town enjoying the day and making plans for an August wedding. Just talking about all of the plans made Brook a little nervous. She knew that she would be rushed trying to plan a wedding, even a small one, in just six months. Eric was very adamant about not having a long engagement and she agreed. They were in love and wanted to be married as soon as possible. She was so into conversation about the wedding that she went right past her turn for Justin's.

"Brook sweetie, you passed the restaurant."

"I know, I did it on purpose. Do you mind if we just go to the park for a minute and talk?"

"Not at all."

The friends walked hand in hand through Piedmont Park until they reached a small pavilion and took a seat on the bench nestled inside.

"Mia, all we have been talking about lately is me, Eric and our wedding. I really didn't mean to be selfish by not asking about you. Tell me what's up with you and David or just you."

"Girl, I thought that you wanted to talk to me about something important. I thought that something had upset you."

"Well, I do want to talk about something important, my best friend. So go ahead, tell me what's up with you."

"Just the usual, you know what's up with work, I've been doing a little shopping, David asked me to marry him and I've been thinking of redecorating my ..."

"What? Stop talking and go back to what you said."

"What did I say?"

"Stop playing with me, Mia, what did you say about David and marriage?"

"Girl, he asked me to go look at engagement rings with him. Thought we should get married."

"Congratulations, Mia. I can't believe that all of us are getting married."

"Slow it down, Brook. You and Tameka are the only ones getting married any time soon."

"I don't understand. You just said that David wants to get married."

"Yeah, but I convinced him that it's too soon for us to take such a huge step."

"But I thought that you loved David. I thought that everything was going great with the two of you."

"I do love him, I love him so much and everything is great between us. I just want to keep it that way. I don't want to rush into something that won't weather the storm. Its better that we take our time and make sure that we're really ready for marriage. Know what I mean?"

"Um yeah, I guess I do." Brook said very hesitantly.

"What's wrong Brook? Why are you looking so funny?"

Brook got up from the bench and started to walk around the pavilion. She never responded to Mia, just kept walking around in that circle with a puzzled look on her face. After about five trips around in a circle, Brook returned to her seat beside Mia.

"I need for you to be completely honest with me Mia. Do you think that I'm rushing into marriage?"

"Do you?"

"Please don't answer my question with a question. I need for you to be honest."

"Well, I honestly think that only you have the answer to that question. Only you know how you feel about Eric and the prospect of being his wife forever. You can't let my feelings about me and David affect you."

"Mia, just answer me damn it! Do you think I'm rushing things?"

"No, Brook! What's gotten into you? You were happy as a lark ten minutes ago and now you're questioning the very thing that was making you so happy. This is why I didn't tell you about David's proposal in the first place. You can't take my way of thinking and make it your own."

"Mia, I don't want to make a mistake."

"Then don't. Don't start questioning what you already know is so right for you. Eric loves you and you love him. You two have been together longer than me and David and you are different people than we are. So be you and do what's right for you."

Brook reached and gave Mia a hug. They then stood up and headed for the car, hand in hand. They giggled at the folks passing by that looked at them with either accusing or curious eyes. Not everyone realized that women could be friends only and hold hands. Holding hands and hugging does not equal lesbian. They reached the car and once again took off to get something to eat.

"Oh my goodness, Mia, I am so sorry."

"For what?"

"We were supposed to be talking about you and I still managed to turn it into a conversation all about me. I am sorry."

"Oh girl please, it's no biggie. I'm always here to listen."

"Yes, but I don't want my need to be heard to keep you from getting what you need out of this friendship."

"Stop tripping, Brook. You're getting married; it is the biggest time in your life."

# CHAPTER TWENTY-SIX

Tameka couldn't deny the fact that she was getting excited about Brook's wedding. It was her hope that she would be able to get some great wedding ideas from Brook without looking like she copied what Brook did. What Tameka was really excited about was the fact that Brook asked her to be her Bridesmaid. Of course Mia was her Maid of Honor, but Tameka also realized that she'd done some things to piss Brook off over the years and she didn't really expect to get the highest honor. Hell, after the knife incident, she didn't expect to get any honor. She continued to sit at the kitchen counter and flip through bridal magazines as she waited for Mia to arrive and Brook to emerge from her bedroom.

Suddenly, a light bulb went off and Tameka decided to put together a quick brunch for them to enjoy as they went over all of Brook's plans. Tameka's little brunch specialty was spicy sausage, hash brown potatoes and eggs. She never told anyone what she did to those sausages, but everyone loved them. The smell of the food cooking drew Brook out of her room sooner than she had planned to drag herself out. She was dressed casually, but still sporting her house shoes. Brook figured what the heck, she was at home so her foot attire really didn't matter.

"Well hello, sleepy head."

"Hi, Tameka. I wasn't asleep in there; I was just lounging and watching television. You know I can't sleep this late."

"I don't know, you got in pretty late last night. I figured Eric had just worn that tail out," Tameka laughed.

"You are so darn crude," Brook replied with a little grin on her face.

"Yeah, I might be crude, but the truth is the light. No point in me trying to sugar coat it or make it sound extra romantic. We're all grown."

"Anyway, what made you decide to cook?"

"Just thought it would be nice to have a little brunch while we all talked. Is that okay with you, or did you have other plans for food?"

"Oh girl, that is fine. You know how much I love those sausages you make. What do you put in them?"

"Brook, you ask me that every time and you get the same answer."

"Yes, I know, it's a family secret."

Brook moved around the island and grabbed a fork. Before Tameka could protest, Brook jabbed a piece of sausage with the utensil and crammed it in her mouth. Immediately Brook dropped the fork and started gasping for air through her mouth. But no amount of huffing and puffing or waving her hand was helping to cool off her mouth. Tameka burst into laughter and leisurely moved about the kitchen and retrieved a glass of ice water. It seemed to Brook as if it took hours for Tameka to give her the water. Brook drank it so fast that water dripped from her mouth onto her shirt. By now Tameka was on the floor with tears rolling down her face and uncontrollable laughter escaping her mouth.

"I guess you're enjoying this." Brook said in a raspy voice.

"Yes I am. Brook, you looked crazy. That will teach you not to eat out of a hot skillet."

"So glad I could provide you with entertainment."

Still laughing, Tameka replied, "Don't get snippy with me, you did this to yourself and you know it's funny as hell."

"Maybe, but you didn't have to laugh so hard. I thought I was going to pass right out."

"Brook, I knew you would be okay and yes, I will laugh about it again as soon as Mia gets here and I can tell her what happened."

"Do me a favor and just don't tell her in front of Toni."

"Who is Toni?"

"I thought I told you, she is my wedding planner and she'll be joining us today."

"Will you give me the eggs out of the fridge? I'd better add another one to the bowl. Make sure I have enough for everyone."

"Here you go. And thanks, Tameka, it's really sweet of you to cook for all of us."

"No problem."

Brook and Tameka were still laughing and talking when they heard the doorbell ring. Brook got up to answer it and was pleased to find Mia standing there looking as beautiful as ever. The two of them greeted one another with a hug and Brook closed the door. They went on into the condo sharing small talk as they made their way to the kitchen.

"Goodness, it smells good in here. Hi Tameka, I see and smell that you're in here throwing down. What are you cooking?"

"Just some eggs, potatoes and sausage."

"Ooh, can I taste one? Those things are so good."

"You may want to wait a minute, they are pretty hot. Aren't they Brook?" Tameka giggled.

"Yes, Miss Smarty Pants, they are very hot."

"Did I miss a joke or something?" Mia asked.

"Yes child, let me tell you….." Tameka was interrupted by the doorbell.

Again, Brook went to the door and let their guest in. She took

Toni's bag and introduced her to both Mia and Tameka. While the food was still piping hot, Tameka laid it all out on the table along with a freshly brewed pot of coffee and a basket of croissants. The four ladies shared small talk and ideas while they consumed the food before them. After everyone was full and satisfied, they cleared the table and began to seriously discuss Brook's wedding plans. Tameka couldn't believe the fabulous suggestions and ideas that Toni was coming up with. It was like getting her own wedding planner for free. She'd already decided that whatever suggestions Brook didn't like, she would just take for herself. Maybe even take some of the ones Brook did like and use. Tameka figured what difference would it make. Brook would get married before her so it wouldn't matter to her what Tameka did for her own ceremony. Three hours later and being completely sure of what she wanted, Brook adjourned the meeting and escorted Toni to the door. There was no doubt in anyone's mind that this would be a dream wedding. Something to be envied by many.

"Wow, Brook, this wedding is going to be fabulous. I can't believe how exquisite the decorations and food will be. When will you tell Eric about the decisions you've made and the cost of it all?" Tameka asked.

"Well, he agreed to leave all of the planning up to me so there is no need for him to be concerned with the cost. But I will share the plans with him later on tonight."

Tameka questioned Brook further as Mia looked on. "You mean he didn't offer to kick in on the cost of this little shindig?"

"Of course he did, but since I can afford it I don't see why I should burden him with the expense."

"Brook," Mia chimed, "don't you think he's going to question the cost when he sees all of the things you've chosen?"

"Yes, he will. That's my biggest dilemma right now. How to let Eric know that I have plenty of money and will take care of the wedding without making him feel as if he can't afford it."

"Hold the hell up," Tameka exclaimed as she jumped to her

feet. "Are you saying that this man doesn't know he is marrying a freaking millionaire?"

"No…he doesn't." Brook responded very cowardly.

Mia just shook her head from side to side in disbelief as Tameka continued to stare at Brook in amazement. Neither of Brook's dear friends could believe that she had agreed to marry a man and start a family with him and never disclose her financial situation. Brook was obviously not thinking clearly. Still staring at Brook intensely,

Tameka begged the question, "Surely you are not going to wait until the day before the wedding to get him to sign the prenuptial agreement? You just can't save that until the last minute, Brook."

"I wasn't going to make him sign one. He's already proven that he's not after my money."

"Damn it, Brook, he can't be after what he doesn't know exists. Come on, get a grip." Tameka shouted.

Brook looked to Mia for some help and support and there was apparently none coming from Mia's direction either.

"Why are you looking at me?" Mia asked.

"Because I know you understand what I'm saying," Brook replied.

"No I don't, Brook, you have got to get these stars out of your eyes long enough to take care of business. We all know that Eric loves you and all of that romantic stuff, but you have to protect your money and future."

"What do you mean future?"

"I'm just saying that no one can be certain about what their future holds. I truly hope that you and Eric will live happily ever after. But if you don't, you need to protect yourself and your financial future. Your parents didn't make all of that money for you to give it away in a divorce settlement."

"But ya'll, I've never even told him that I am wealthy or even comfortable. He just thinks that I make a good living from my job and that I'm good at handling my finances. How do I tell him now that he's marrying an heiress?"

"I don't know," chimed Tameka, "but you need to find the words immediately."

"I couldn't agree more," added Mia.

# CHAPTER TWENTY-SEVEN

Brook found it almost impossible to concentrate on her work. She was making simple errors on simple work issues that would have management questioning whether she was in her right mind. These are things that she would have to correct prior to handing this project over. They just wouldn't be corrected today. Brook felt that if she could just finish the project today she would be in a better place mentally to make all of the corrections tomorrow. If she could just get through this talk with Eric tonight she would be better off mentally to do a lot of things that needed to be done.

"Brook. Brook." Mia called as she tapped her friend on the shoulder.

"Oh, hi Mia. What's up?"

"What are you thinking about? You seem a million miles away."

"Well, you know I'm having my little talk with Eric tonight. Mia, I'm so nervous, I don't even know how to begin."

"Brook, you'll just have to spit it out. You have to tell this man the truth. Have you had the pre-nup drawn up yet?"

"No, I thought I'd wait to see his reaction first."

"Fine, but don't romanticize everything to the point that you don't protect yourself."

"Do you really believe that Eric would try to take my money if something happened?"

"Sweetie, I'd like to think not, but I'm sure Nichole didn't think that O.J. would kill her either. The point is that we can't predict the future and you have to ultimately protect yourself." With that said Mia gave Brook a kiss on the cheek and returned to her office.

Brook left work and headed over to Eric's. He'd offered to cook her a nice dinner tonight and she felt that this would be the best time to go ahead and spill her guts about her fortune. As she drove through the city to his house she contemplated just how she would tell him and tried to imagine what his response would be. Would he be angry that she hadn't told him before? Would he jump up and down as if he'd just hit lotto? Before Brook knew it she was sitting in front of his house just staring at the front door. She sat there so long that he came to the car and knocked on the window signaling for her to unlock the door. She opened the car door, stood up and gave her man a hug. They walked on in the house hand in hand.

"Baby, I know I'm not a gourmet cook, but was the food that bad? You hardly ate and you've barely said two words since you got here. Is everything okay?"

"Eric sweetie, I have something on my mind, something I need to talk to you about."

"Sounds serious."

"Kind of, you mind if we go into the den and talk?"

"Not at all," Eric responded as he got up and pulled Brook's chair out for her. He led her by the hand to the sofa.

"Okay, baby, what's on your mind? Does it have anything to do with the wedding?"

"Somewhat. Maybe it has more to do with the marriage. You know our finances."

"Brook baby, you know I'm not a wealthy man, but I make a

very good living. My salary along with savings, stocks and bonds should allow us to live pretty comfortably. And I promise that someday I'll be able to buy you your ultimate dream house. I will take care of you."

"Eric, I'm not worried about your finances. I know that you do well and would care for me. What we need to talk about are my finances."

"What's wrong, baby, have you over extended yourself. I know that that condo of yours has to run you a few thousand a month."

"Eric, please just listen. My condo is paid for; I paid for it out right. Remember I told you that when my parents died they left me a little money."

"Yes I remember."

"Well, baby, they left me a little more than I led you to believe."

"No kidding, I can't believe you own that condo."

"Well, with the sale of my father's business and other monies that they left me, I have several million dollars," Brook confessed as her voice trailed off.

"Several million?" Eric asked.

"Yes, Eric, several million. If it were my desire, I could just travel the world and never work again."

"So why don't you, why are you here with me and not with someone in your own tax bracket?"

"Because I love you, baby. I don't care about tax brackets or your portfolio. I care about you and the way you love me."

"I love you too, Brook and you know that. But how will you feel long term about being with a man that can never do for you what you can do for yourself?"

"Eric, you have already done for me what no one else ever could. You treat me like a queen, love like no man ever has and do things to my body that drive me crazy. You do things for me that no amount of money could ever buy."

"I'm glad that you feel that way now, Brook, but will it be enough in the years to come?"

"Something you need to understand, Eric is that money does not make you a man. You proved to me a long time ago that you were more of a man than so many others that I know. You take care of your mama; you've planned very well for your own financial future. You're a God fearing man that leads a good, clean and respectable life. Isn't that enough for you?"

"Yes, but is it enough for you. I know that you say these things now, but will it still be enough ten years from now?"

"Eric, you are all that I need for the rest of my life. I just need for you to always be the man that you are today."

Eric turned to his bride-to-be and looked at her so tenderly. He truly loved this woman but for the first time he wondered if he would be enough for her. He wondered if her money would ever drive a wedge between them. Brook raised her hand to Eric's face and stroked it gently as if to ease his worries. She leaned in to kiss him on the cheek. That small kiss turned into a very passionate one and that passionate one turned into a night of breath-taking sex. The following morning as the two of them got ready for work Eric decided he'd share the thought that he'd pondered all night.

"Baby."

"Yes, Eric, what is it?"

"We need to go to your attorney's office sometime this week to have a prenuptial agreement drawn up."

"Eric, I didn't tell you about my wealth for that reason. I just thought that you should know before we were married."

"I know, Brook, but business is still business. I need for you to know that no matter what happens between us, good or bad, that your finances are protected."

"You think we'll ever fall apart?"

"Hell no, baby girl. This is just business, you are stuck with me forever!" Eric exclaimed as he picked her up and planted a kiss right on her lips.

Across town, Mia was preparing breakfast for she and David. They had decided to go into work late and spend the morning together. It was David's idea that they go out for breakfast and enjoy a little time together. Needless to say, he was pleasantly surprised to find Mia preparing ham and cheese omelets, coffee and fresh squeezed juice. When she went to set the food on the table, Mia found tulips, her favorite flowers, sitting on her place mat. That gesture touched her heart and made her day. Anyone can buy roses, but it's really special when a man takes the time to ask and remember your favorite things.

"So Mia, do you have a busy day ahead?"

"No, not really. Just tying up some loose ends on a project. What about you?"

"Nothing so pressing that I can't take a little time to spend with my baby."

"Well aren't you sweet."

"I can't help myself."

"Well, Mr. I can't help myself, what did you do last night?"

"A client gave me tickets to a Braves game so me and another co-worker went. I called Eric to see if he wanted to hang, but he already had plans with Brook."

"Yeah, I'm sure that they had an interesting night."

"What do you mean by that?"

"Well, Mr. Nosey, Brook was supposed to have a talk about her finances with Eric."

"Sounds exciting." David mumbled sarcastically.

"I bet it was interesting once she told him that she's actually a multi millionaire."

"A what?"

"You heard me, smart guy. But please don't say anything and when Eric tells you, please pretend to be surprised."

Eric and Mia went on with their conversation and breakfast. When they realized how late it was getting, they jumped up, kissed one another and headed off to work.

# CHAPTER TWENTY-EIGHT

The car was whipped into its assigned parking space and Tameka jumped out ready to conquer another day. She had been floating on air ever since she took over the anchor position. She was receiving more attention from strangers than she'd ever really expected. Finally, she was experiencing a little of the celebrity status that she'd only dreamed of. She had accepted the position on a permanent basis and a hefty little pay raise to go along with it.

Mr. Thomas, the station manager, never expected Tameka to be as well received as she was. It was as if the public was magnetically drawn to her. Tameka's noon day broadcast was really starting to give the other three major stations a run for their money. Mr. Thomas knew it wouldn't be long before those other stations began trying to court Tameka away from him. He could only hope for now that his continuous praise and that salary increase would keep her happy.

As Tameka walked through the garage on her way to the elevator, she could have sworn that she heard footsteps behind her. She turned to look, but there was no one. Feeling a little uneasy, she picked up her pace and didn't take the time to look back again. Just as she arrived at the elevator and pushed the button, Monica appeared right in front of her face. Monica's clothes were disheveled and she looked as if she hadn't slept in days.

"I guess you're pretty proud of yourself, you job stealing bitch. I know that you planted those damn drugs on me and soon enough I'll be able to prove it."

"Monica, you really need to get it together, you look an absolute mess. You'll never regain your position if you don't get off of that stuff and clean yourself up."

"Bitch, you know I'm not on anything! I ought to kill you now for ruining my life. With your fucking lie following me, I can't get a job at any other station. But you better believe that I will make your raggedy ass pay."

"Monica, get help."

Tameka stepped into the elevator and as the doors closed she could still hear Monica shouting obscenities at her. Tameka never meant to completely ruin Monica's career, but she could no longer allow herself to be treated like dirt by the likes of Monica. She could not allow anyone to think that they were somehow better than she was. Once she arrived in the office, Tameka went straight to Mr. Thomas and told him of her verbal assault. He assured her that security would be beefed up and she would be protected at all times while on company property.

By the time Tameka made it back to her car after work, her windshield had been busted and all four tires slashed. Her beautiful car was now covered with filthy words written with bright orange spray paint. Words like bitch, slut and Satan smeared what she used to call her baby. She was more hurt and embarrassed than angry and worried how she would explain this to Wayne.

After Tameka had her car towed away and had Wayne take her to pick up a rental, she was exhausted. All she wanted was to go home, take a long bath and go to bed. Unfortunately, she'd allowed Wayne to convince her to spend the night with him. She knew that he would want to know all the details leading up to her car being trashed. As she pulled into the driveway behind Wayne, Tameka took a deep breath and tried to mentally prepare herself for a night of questions. But to Tameka's surprise Wayne didn't immediately start questioning her. He instead ran her a hot bath and prepared dinner while she soaked.

"Feeling better?" Wayne asked.

"Definitely! Thanks baby."

"Are you hungry? I fixed a great buffalo chicken salad."

"That sounds wonderful, Wayne."

Tameka filled a couple of glasses with soda and sat down at the table. Wayne sat down and served the salads. They ate in silence for what seemed like a lifetime. Tameka knew that he was dying to ask her about her day and all that happened but was trying hard to restrain himself.

"Go ahead, baby."

"Go ahead and what, Tameka?"

"Let's just get this out of the way. Go ahead and ask me what happened."

"Okay, what happened today, baby? Why would someone trash your car like that?"

"It was Monica. She obviously hasn't gotten over the fact that I'm the anchor now."

"But why take her frustrations out on you, why not the station manager?"

"Well, she has it in her head that I set her up to be fired."

"Tameka, please stop beating around the bush. Why would she blame you, what actually caused her to be fired? I've asked before but never got a straight answer and now this has happened. Please clearly answer my questions."

"Wayne, the day that Monica was fired we were getting ready to go to lunch with Mr. Thomas. I accidently bumped into Monica and her purse fell to the floor. Mr. Thomas picked up a vile of crack that fell out with all of her other things. She thinks that I dropped the drugs to make it look like it was hers. She wants revenge when she needs to be concentrating on getting help. You should've seen her today, she looked a mess."

"So you actually saw her do this to your car?"

"No, but she was there when I got in this morning. She ran up to me in the garage spewing venom and threatening to pay me back for setting her up. She wants to blame me for her inability to get another job. I swear she's unstable."

Wayne leaned back in his chair and ran his hands over his head as if the weight of the world was on his shoulders. He took a deep sigh and stared at Tameka as if he could see right through her.

"Why are you looking at me like that?" Tameka asked.

"Be honest with me, Tameka, did you do it? Did you plant the drugs?"

"I can't believe you would even fix your mouth to ask me some bullshit like that."

"Please don't curse, it's so un-lady like."

"Wayne, I can talk however the fuck I want to. How do you like that word?"

"Why can't you just answer my question, did you do it?"

"I don't need this, I'm going home."

Tameka pushed away from the table and headed out of the kitchen. Before she could make it through the doorway she was stopped in her tracks by Wayne's words.

"I saw a vile with a rock in it in your purse a little while back. I wasn't sure what it was, but refused to even let myself think it could be drugs."

Tameka spun around. "What were you doing in my bag?"

"I was getting your keys so that I could go and put gas in the car for you. Remember you said you didn't want to have to stop at the station the next morning?"

Tameka was completely dumb struck. She stood there with her mouth open and her eyes glued to Wayne's back. What would she tell him now? If he knew that she had in fact planted the drugs, would he still love her, still marry her?

"Why don't you come on back over here, sit down and talk to me."

Tameka slowly walked back to the table and took her seat. She held her head down as if she were preparing to be punished by her father.

"Where did you get the drugs, Tameka?"

"My brother."

"Why, why would you do that to Monica?"

"Baby, you weren't there, I just couldn't take her humiliating me anymore. I was tired of her always putting me down or trying to degrade me in front of everyone. I can't allow anyone to think that they are superior to me."

"Okay, Tameka, you've got to give me more than this. This is the first time you've ever even mentioned her treating you badly. I always thought that she was perfectly nice to you, a little nosey or annoying maybe, but never mean to you."

"Well, she was mean and nasty the day after we got engaged. First she congratulates me and then holds my hand in the air and talks about my ring as if it came out of a Cracker Jack box. She tried to humiliate me in front of everyone."

"So you hadn't already planned to use the drugs you were carrying around?"

"Okay Wayne, I had thought about planting them so I could get a shot at the anchor desk. I'd decided not to hurt her just to get my chance but after her little stunt I couldn't help myself."

Wayne sat quietly for a while. He eventually got up and started to clear the dishes from the table. He moved about the kitchen wondering just how much he really knew about his fiancé. Wayne realized a long time ago that Tameka had a horrible temper, but never imagined she was capable of these type of things. He loved her dearly, but had to question what he was really getting into.

"Are you not going to talk to me anymore? I know what I did was bad, Wayne, but it was like I just couldn't stop myself. I was so angry at that moment that I just wanted my revenge."

"So you kill two birds with one stone. You get Monica back and a shot at the anchor job."

"You make me sound like some diabolical psychopath."

Wayne walked over to Tameka, kneeled in front of her and held her hands. He looked deeply into her eyes trying to see if there was some kind of monster hiding deep inside. All he saw was the woman he loved.

"Tameka, I love you baby and I know that you are not a psychopath. However, I do worry about you and the way you treat folks sometimes. I don't want you hurt because someone tries to pay you back. You have to work on how you deal with your anger baby."

"I know and I promise to do better. I'm sure that I've seen the last of Monica. She's paid me back and now I'm sure she feels that she can move on."

"I hope you're right."

# CHAPTER TWENTY-NINE

The ESPN Zone was a little more crowded than David had anticipated. He walked around and surveyed the place before taking a seat at a small table in the corner. He ordered a pitcher of beer and admired the scenery as the waitress walked away from his table. The place was full of beautiful, fine women that had their assets on display for all of the men to admire. Whether they were purposefully flaunting or not, they all looked good to David. If he hadn't been waiting for Eric to join him, he would have sat at the bar so that he could have a clear, unobstructed view of the entire place.

David wondered if Eric had learned that he was marrying a millionaire yet. They hadn't had a chance to really talk in a while so when David suggested they get together after work, Eric immediately agreed. Mia had sworn him to secrecy so he couldn't bring up anything concerning money but he sure hoped that Eric would. The waitress returned with the pitcher of beer and a couple of glasses. After placing everything on the table she took David's food order of wings and fries. This way he and Eric wouldn't have to wait long for food once Eric arrived. As the waitress repeated the order back to David, he eyeballed every inch of her body. She walked away and he shook his head in disbelief. He couldn't believe how gorgeous she was.

"Man, you've got drool running down your chin." Eric said with laughter as he sat down.

"Eric, did you see how fine she was? It makes no sense for her to look so good."

"I thought Mia was the best looking thing you'd ever seen."

"Yeah, she is, but that doesn't make me blind to every other fine woman."

"I hear you. How long have you been here?"

"Not long at all. I went ahead and got us some wings, is that cool with you?"

"Yeah."

The two men sat and talked about work, sports and other meaningless conversation until their food arrived.

"David, man, I like spicy food too but these wings are about to blow my head off."

"Stop complaining man and eat up. Besides, you need something like this every now and then to put hair on your chest."

"Hell, my chest is hairy enough."

Eric managed to get a couple more wings down and finished his beer. He leaned back in his chair and took in his surroundings. David could tell by his demeanor that he was getting ready to talk about something serious.

"David, have you kept any secrets from Mia since you two have been dating?"

"No, I really don't have any. Why do you ask?"

"I found out that Brook had been keeping a hell of a secret from me."

"Oh yeah, care to elaborate?"

"She's a millionaire. I'm getting to ready to marry a millionaire."

"My man Eric, when you do it, you do it right. But why did it take Brook so long to tell you?"

"She said she didn't know how. I think that part of her

wanted to make sure that I wanted her for her and not for what she has. She still seemed kind of hesitant to tell me."

"So what did you say, how do you respond to something like that?"

"You offer to sign a pre-nup."

"You what! I know you aren't serious. Tell me you are not signing away your chance at millions."

"I already did. I figure I didn't know anything about it from the start and wanted to marry her so it really shouldn't matter now. The money changes nothing, it's Brook I want."

"Well, don't you sound whipped."

"Screw you man. That money was left to her by her parents, they didn't intend for anyone else to have it. That includes her future husband."

"Man, I just wish you had waited a little while and thought about it. Maybe you shouldn't have been so fast to sign everything away."

"I've supported myself all these years, I can keep on. Besides, I don't want my woman taking care of me. Of course, now we'll have things that we wouldn't have had if it was all up to me, but I still want to carry my share of the load."

"I hear you and I can respect that, man."

"Thanks."

"Hey Eric, don't we know that girl that just walked in over there?"

Tameka was standing near the front entrance looking like a million bucks. She had put in a couple of extra hours at the office working on a spotlight story to air later in the month. A co-worker had convinced Tameka to ride with her to grab a bite to eat. They were seated a couple of minutes after arriving and David never took his eyes off of her. He couldn't quite remember where he knew her from and then it hit him.

"Eric, man, that's the news anchor from CNN. I knew I'd seen her somewhere."

"David, you met her long before she was on CNN. That's

the chick that tried to throw herself at you on Christmas. Remember you were into Mia and Tameka was into you."

"Oh yeah, I remember now. That girl was a trip."

The next thing everyone knew, there was a short woman dressed in black running up to Tameka's table. To Tameka's horror it was Monica. She had obviously followed Tameka and she came in the door shouting obscenities and directing them all at Tameka.

"This is a stealing, lying, conniving whore. Any man interested in her had better think twice because I hear the bitch has AIDS."

Tameka jumped up and attempted to shove Monica away from her table. When that didn't work she called for security. Monica continued her ranting.

"You are a stinking, evil bitch, Tameka and I hope you burn in hell! I hope someone snatches your ass up and beats all hell out of you, you freaking slut!"

Monica was still screaming at the top of her lungs as security threw her out the door. Tameka was embarrassed beyond belief. David and Eric were still in the corner laughing themselves silly. When they finally stopped laughing long enough to look up again, Tameka was gone.

# CHAPTER THIRTY

The Cathedral was breath-taking. Brook had always admired the church, but didn't expect the inside to be as gorgeous as it was. It was definitely where she and Eric would be married. Of course the church wouldn't even be one fourth full because it seated a few thousand people. But as long as Brook was surrounded by the people she loved and that loved her, she would be completely happy. Today she was glad to have Mia and Tameka with her. She had met Eric at the church weeks earlier to make sure that it was okay with Him, but wanted to come back with her girls to get their opinions as well. It tickled her pink to see them as excited and blown away as she was.

After leaving the church the three friends headed further into town to pick up menu options from the Georgian Terrace. The reception would be held there and once Brook and Eric narrowed down their food choices, the items would be prepared for them and served at a private tasting. That is when they would make their final menu choices. But no matter what was served, it would seem phenomenal just because of the surroundings. The elegant white room with the lavish curtains and chandeliers. Brook could hardly wait to become Eric's wife. Mrs. Brook Mansfield-Banks, damn that sounded good.

"Alright, ladies, I want to thank you for your patience and support through all of this. Now, how about some dinner?"

"Is it just me or does it seem like we are always going somewhere to eat?" Tameka quizzed.

"Yes, we do go out to eat a lot, but I like it. It gives us a chance to talk and spend some girl time together." responded Mia.

Out of curiosity, Brook asked, "Is there something you would rather be doing?"

"Maybe we should try going to a club every now and then. You know dance a little bit, drink a little bit."

"Get harassed by gold tooth, broke brothers a little bit." Mia added with a chuckle.

"I don't know, Tameka, a piano bar or restaurant with a band I don't mind. But I'm just not into the club thing; it's just not for me." Brook admitted.

"Ya'll are so boring. Like two little old ladies. I think I'll give you Geritol for your wedding gift, Brook."

"Ha-ha, Tameka's got jokes. You can pick at me all you want, but tonight your tail is going to dinner. So hush your mouth and enjoy the free meal."

"Oh she got you told." Mia blurted out in laughter."

The Goldfish restaurant was pretty full but they were still able to get in without a long wait. Once seated, they ordered up a small feast, a little bit of everything so they could share. They toasted to their friendship, pending nuptials and the men in their lives.

"I don't want to break anyone's good mood, but Tameka can I ask you about something, a rumor I heard?" Brook asked.

"Sure, ask away."

"What happened with you and Monica Greer in the ESPN Zone the other day?"

"How did you hear about that?" Tameka quizzed.

"Eric and David were there and saw everything, but I'm trying to figure out what started it all."

"I guess you want to know too, huh?" Tameka asked Mia.

"Well if you're offering up the story I'm sure ready to listen."

Tameka didn't even feel like beating around the bush or covering up what she had done to provoke the situation with her and Monica, so she just came clean. Told them everything about the drugs and Monica losing her job. They were shocked to find out that sweet looking Monica was capable of getting so angry. First trashing the car and then the ESPN Zone incident. Seeing someone on the news gives you no insight as to what type of person they really are. Seeing how Tameka is on the news every day would never lead anyone to believe that she could do the things that she does. Mia and Brook looked at one another in disbelief for what seemed like an eternity.

"Are you all going to say anything or just sit there and stare at each other forever?"

"Tameka, I'm honestly at a loss for words. I don't understand how you could so easily decide to ruin that woman's life." Brook said with her voice tinged with disgust.

"Gee, Brook, just tell me how you really feel." Tameka responded defensively.

"Well, Tameka, I will tell you how I feel. You can't honestly think that you can do something to someone like that and think that they will just accept it. You'll be lucky if Monica doesn't try to kill you. She worked hard to get that position and you took it away with one fatal blow."

"Brook, what about what she did to me. Would you like to be humiliated in front of your entire office?" Tameka was almost shouting.

"No matter what she said in front of the office, Tameka, she didn't deserve that. You've got to learn to just let some things go and not always think in terms of revenge."

"Would both of you calm down. You're drawing attention to our table." Mia stated very firmly.

"Is that all you have to say, Mia, calm down? As much as you hate me I thought you'd take this opportunity to jump all over me."

"First of all, Tameka, I don't hate you and I don't have to jump all over you. I realized a long time ago that everything you put out into the universe comes back to you. So I'll just warn you to be careful because if you keep putting these bad things out there, you're going to have one hurtful boomerang coming back your way. Now, can we drop this and try to enjoy the rest of our evening?"

"Fine," snapped Tameka.

For the next half hour they sat there and ate, drank and shared very meaningless conversation. Those thirty minutes felt more like two hours. Tired of playing like everything was alright, Brook asked for and paid the check. They all went back to Brook's car and headed to her condo. Once in the parking garage, Tameka wasted no time jumping out of Brook's car and heading straight for her's.

"Are you not coming up, Tameka?" Brook asked.

"No, I decided to spend the night with Wayne. I'll see you sometime tomorrow."

With that, Tameka was gone and Brook asked Mia to come up and talk for a while. Mia didn't hesitate because she had some things that she wanted to tell Brook. Mia felt that it was time for Brook to get her priorities in order as far as Tameka was concerned. It didn't take Brook and Mia any time to get comfortable on the family room floor with tea and cookies. Yes, they had just eaten, but this was their ritual whenever they wanted to share serious conversation.

"Okay, Brook, you'll be married very soon. What do you plan to do about this condo and have you told Tameka that she'll have to leave once you are married?"

"Me and Eric decided to move me into his house. It's nice and cozy and it seems to be what he really prefers. At least until we have a new house built."

"That didn't answer my question."

"Well, Tameka won't be getting married until sometime next year and she asked if she could lease the place from me."

"And you said?"

"I told her that I'd have a new lease agreement drawn up and if she agreed to the terms I'd let her stay."

"What in the world are you thinking? When you leave she needs to leave with you. She can afford to buy her own house. Make her stop mooching off of you."

"She's not mooching, Mia, she'll be paying her own way. Besides, this will keep me from having to put it on the market or lease to someone that I really don't know. I know that she'll take care of the place."

"And if she doesn't?"

"Mia, I have her putting down a pretty hefty security deposit. One that she won't want to lose."

"So you are not afraid that you'll end up losing money on this place?"

"No, because I paid for it straight out. Any money I get for rent is all profit and she is responsible for all of the utilities and trust me, the utilities will all be in her name."

"I still just don't see why she won't get her own place. You could make a small fortune off of this condo and I know she's not paying you what you could get for rent."

"Yes, I could get more but I don't mind. I would do the same for you."

"I know you would, Brook, but the difference is that I wouldn't ask you to. I would never take advantage of our friendship. And while I'm on my little soap box, you do know that she's just gathering all of the info she can from your wedding plans so that she can use them herself."

"Yes, I know that I'll see a lot of my things in her wedding. I figured that one out a long time ago."

"I swear, Brook, you are just too nice for your own good. That girl is really going to hurt you one day and you won't even see it coming because of those rose colored glasses you're wearing."

"Don't say that Mia."

"Well the truth is the light Brook. I just want you to be on guard."

Brook and Mia talked a while longer before Mia decided she'd better get moving. She was supposed to be meeting David at her place around 10:00pm and didn't want to keep him waiting. She gave Brook a hug and headed out the door leaving Brook to ponder all of her warnings. Thirty-five minutes later she was walking through her door and before she could close it, David walked in behind her.

"I missed you, baby." David said seductively and followed it with a kiss.

"I missed you too. Come on in and I'll show you just how much."

"Can't turn down an offer like that now can I?"

"A wise man wouldn't."

David wasn't patient enough to make it to the bedroom. He had his way with his woman on the den floor. After regaining their composure and breath, they gathered their things and headed for the bedroom. David tried to pull Mia into bed, but instead she coerced him into a hot, steamy shower. They washed one another and David even took the time to wash Mia's hair for her. He then dried her off, lotioned her down and dressed her for bed. Mia adored the way he took care of her.

"Thank you, sweetie."

"Anytime."

"I'm going to fix a cup of cocoa, would you like some?"

"Sure, that sounds good. Do you have any of those little cookies I like?"

"Yes sir, I'll bring you some back."

Mia went into the kitchen and returned a few minutes later with their goodies. She sat down on the bed and placed the tray between her and David. They shared the events of their day and

Mia shared with David the story behind the ESPN Zone incident that he witnessed.

"Mia baby, you and Brook really know how to pick the crazies to be friends with."

"I didn't pick her. I got stuck with her by way of Brook. But she knows that she is not really one of my favorite people. I don't trust her and don't think that Brook should either."

"Baby, I know that you love Brook and want to protect her, but sometimes you just have to let people learn the hard way."

"I guess."

# CHAPTER THIRTY-ONE

Craig was beyond surprised when he learned that Tameka had permanently taken over the noon day spot from Monica. He had seen her filling in on television but it wasn't until he returned to work that he learned the change was forever. He questioned a couple of co-workers as to what prompted the change and was shocked to hear that it was because of Monica's alleged drug use. As soon as he was told what transpired the day of Monica's dismissal, he knew something wasn't right. He smelled a rat and it smelled an awful lot like Tameka.

After a few days, Craig managed to get his hands on Monica's personnel record and copied her number and address. He had to talk with her in person, that talk took place a couple of weeks ago and he and Monica had been inseparable every since. Monica was comforted by Craig and his belief that Tameka had set her up to lose her job. He shared with Monica what Tameka did to him and how the lack of evidence allowed her to walk around scot free.

"So, baby, do you promise that we'll get her back? And if so, when? I want that bitch to pay now."

"I know, Monica, but we have to do this right, or we'll be

the ones in jail and Tameka will still be parading around like the queen of the universe. You're going to have to be patient, baby."

Monica kicked the covers off and rolled over on top of Craig. She kissed him deeply and started working her way down his body with her tongue. She wrapped her arms around his waist and did that thing he had come to love so much. The girl could definitely work magic with her mouth and he couldn't get enough of her. Monica pulled away from Craig and rolled over pulling him onto her. He knew how Monica liked it a little rough and was more than willing to please her.

"Harder," she moaned as Craig moved in and out, in and out and picked up speed and strength with each motion of his hips. Drenched in perspiration he collapsed onto the bed with a smile on his face.

"You are incredible," Monica softly whispered in his ear.

"Baby, we are incredible together."

By the time Craig got out of the shower and finished dressing for work, Monica had breakfast waiting for him. She loved taking care of him. It was her way of showing her appreciation for all of the support he'd given her. No one else had even bothered to give her the benefit of the doubt when it came to the so called drug issue. Many of her friends didn't even bother to return her calls once she had lost her job under such horrible circumstances. But Craig was there for her and vowed to help her get her revenge on Tameka.

"Monica, everything smells great and goodness knows I could eat a bear."

"Well pull up a seat and enjoy."

Monica was quiet for a moment, but couldn't resist asking Craig the questions that she already knew his answers to. "Baby, when are we going to start making Tameka pay? I don't know how much longer I can wait. I want her to suffer the way she's made me suffer. I'm tired of seeing her on television everyday enjoying the life I worked so hard for."

"I know, Monica, but you're going to have to be patient. We

have to be careful in all that we do. You don't want her getting the upper hand again. Just trust me, she'll pay. And please remember, no more stunts like the one you pulled at ESPN. We don't need to give anyone any reason to suspect you of anything. So just chill baby, it will happen."

"Yeah, whatever you say."

Craig could detect the disappointment in her voice but he had to try and keep Monica from doing anything stupid. The truth was that Craig had no intentions of trying to make Tameka pay. Over the last two weeks he had really come to care for Monica and let go of any ideas he had about revenge. He knew that in the end, Tameka would get what was coming to her, but now he had to keep Monica from creating more problems for herself. He had to somehow convince her to forget about Tameka and concentrate on their relationship and rebuilding her career.

"Are you finished eating?"

"Yeah, baby, that was good. So after you finish with your interview you're going to swing back by the station and pick me up for lunch?"

"Yes, that's the plan." Monica said with no emotion.

Craig grabbed his things and walked up and kissed Monica. "Don't be angry, baby; remember I'm on your side." He then took her by the hand and they headed out the door.

# CHAPTER THIRTY-TWO

"Can you believe that I only have three weeks left as a single woman?" Brook asked Tameka as she finished off her morning cup of coffee.

"I know, the time is flying by. Before you know it, you'll be married with six kids and driving car pool to school."

"Okay, let's not get crazy. I'd better get out of here. So remember, I'm only working a half day and I'll be by your job at 1:30 to pick you up. The attorney's office is right around the corner from the station so you won't be gone from work very long."

"You think we'll be able to get in and out within an hour?"

"Sure. I'll see you later."

Brook picked up her brief case and headed out the door. Tameka sat at the breakfast bar a while longer wondering how detailed this new lease agreement would be. She hadn't really thought that Brook would make her sign a new lease but she was very wrong. Brook was all about business when it came to discussions about Tameka remaining in the condo once she was married and gone. That's why she had volunteered to pick Tameka up today and drive her to the attorney's office to review and sign the new lease. Brook didn't want to give Tameka the opportunity to say that she got caught up at work and had to miss the appointment.

Tameka took her last sip of coffee and left for work herself. The drive into town was surprisingly smooth. There wasn't nearly as much traffic as usual and Tameka was grateful for that. She parked her car and headed for the elevator. It was just her luck that she entered the elevator right behind Craig. She was disgusted that he was back at work. It was her hope that he would never return.

"Good morning, Tameka."

"Hey," Tameka responded sharply.

"Why so angry, did someone piss in your cornflakes this morning?"

"Craig, I don't understand why you are even speaking to me. Why are you back here?"

"Well, I'm back here because I need my job and I won't allow you to take that from me. I'm speaking because it's the polite thing to do."

The elevator doors opened and Tameka couldn't wait to step out. Craig stepped out behind her and wished her a good day. Tameka just rolled her eyes and went straight into her office. For the life of her, Tameka couldn't figure out what Craig was up to. She couldn't understand why he was being so pleasant to her. He had to be up to something. But whatever it was, Tameka couldn't concern herself with it now. She had to go over her copy and get with the producer about what stories were definitely in for the noon day report and which ones would have to be cut.

The day was flying by and before she realized it, it was 1:28 and she knew that Brook was already waiting for her in the parking garage. Tameka grabbed her purse and ran for the elevator. Sure enough, she saw Brook standing outside of the car talking on her cell phone when the elevator doors opened. Brook waived at her and as Tameka started walking toward the car she was spotted by someone else.

Monica was sitting with her car running waiting for Craig to come down for lunch when she saw Tameka strutting across the garage. She was instantly filled with rage and without thinking; she hit the gas and pointed the car directly at Tameka. Brook heard the screeching tires and on instinct started running toward Tameka shouting for her to get out of the way. As the car got closer, Brook pushed Tameka out of the way, then everything went dark.

"Oh my God, someone please help me. Call 911!" Tameka heard herself screaming.

Craig stepped off the elevator and heard someone crying and screaming. He ran over to see Tameka kneeling over Brook. "What happened?"

"Someone hit her, they ran her down," Tameka sobbed. "Oh God, they tried to hit me, who would want to kill me?"

"Have you called the police?"

"Yes."

"Tameka, did you get a look at the car?" Did you see who was driving?"

"No, I saw a black car, but they never slowed down."

Within minutes the police and ambulance were on the scene. While the paramedics cared for Brook and loaded her into the ambulance, the police questioned Tameka. But she was too hysterical to answer anything. Craig told them what he knew and then volunteered to drive Tameka to the hospital so that she could be with her friend. While in route, Tameka called Mia and Eric and told them that Brook had been hurt and that they needed to get the hospital quick.

Eric arrived shortly before Mia and had been listening in on the conversation between the police and Tameka. Once Mia arrived, Craig introduced himself to her and Eric and proceeded to tell them what he knew. He answered their questions as best he could and then returned to his seat beside Tameka.

Everyone waited for what seemed like an eternity to get an update on Brook's condition. Finally a doctor came into the waiting room and delivered the news.

"She is one lucky lady. She has a mild concussion and some pretty deep bruising, but all in all, Miss Mansfield should be fine. We'll keep her overnight for observation and then she can continue to recuperate at home."

"And you're sure she'll be fine? Brook will suffer no long term effects?" Eric asked anxiously.

"No sir, she should make a full and complete recovery within a couple of weeks. I do suggest that she stay home and get plenty of rest over the next week or so."

"Thank you, doctor, thank you so much." Eric was so relieved.

The doctor turned to leave and stopped for a moment, "I almost forgot, she did ask to see Eric and Mia."

Brook's best friend and fiancé followed the doctor to her room leaving Tameka and Craig behind. When they entered the room Brook was laying there with her eyes closed. Eric walked to her bed side and took her hand in his and Brook instantly opened her eyes. She looked up and smiled at Eric.

"I must look a mess."

"Oh, sweetie, you are still just as beautiful as ever. I was so scared when Tameka called me. I didn't know what to expect. But I'm so relieved to know that you're going to be okay."

"Is Mia here?"

Mia walked to the bed and kissed her friend on the forehead. "Hey, girl, who gave you permission to scare the crap out of us?" Mia asked with a smile.

"I didn't mean to scare anyone. I'm not even sure of what happened. How did I end up here?"

"You decided to play superwoman." Mia stated with a slight smile.

"What do you mean?"

"Well, apparently someone in a black car tried to run Tameka down. When you saw what was happening, you ran and pushed her out of the way and the car hit you."

Eric let go of Brook's hand and walked over to the window.

Both Brook and Mia could tell that something was weighing heavily on his mind. However, neither had to guess what it was, they knew he was upset about Tameka. With much hesitation in her voice, Brook finally asked, "What is it baby?"

"Brook," Eric started in a very firm voice, "you've got to let that girl go. She is nothing but trouble, always has been and always will be. She was almost the death of you, baby. I want that poison out of your life!"

The door swung open and in walked Tameka. "Nice to know that you think so highly of me, Eric. You act like I intentionally hurt Brook. I would never do anything to cause her this kind of pain."

"Now is not the time, Tameka." Mia stated matter-of-factly.

"Well when is the time, Mia? I'm tired of always being talked about and ragged on."

"I said not now, Tameka. I think you should go now. We'll get with you later. Good-bye."

"Brook, if you need me, I'll be in the waiting room." Tameka turned and left.

Eric shook his head in disgust. He could only hope that this would be the final straw for Brook and she would see Tameka as the cancer she was and cut her out of her life.

"You all know that she is not the one that hit me," Brook said shyly.

"But it was someone's hatred for her that put you in harm's way. If she were a decent human being no one would want to run her down" Eric replied angrily.

The hospital room door opened once again and the doctor entered. He advised Eric and Mia that Brook really needed her rest and they should step out for a while or just come back tomorrow.

"Brook, baby, I'll be right outside. I'll come back in as soon as they'll let me. I love you." Eric kissed Brooks hand and he and Mia left the room. Both were disgusted to see Tameka still sitting in the waiting area.

"So, Tameka, who wants you dead?" Mia asked sharply.

"How the hell am I supposed to know?"

"You mean you've pissed off so many people that you can't narrow it down to one or two that might want to cause you harm?"

"No, Mia, I haven't pissed anyone off. I have no idea who would want to see me dead. And why can't you have a little sympathy for me, I'm the one in danger. Do you know how scary it is to know that someone is gunning for you."

"Forgive me for not giving a damn about you right now."

"Ladies," Craig called out, "this arguing isn't going to resolve a thing. I think it best that I get you home, Tameka, and you can see Brook tomorrow."

Craig helped Tameka to her feet and escorted her out to her car. He put her in the passenger seat and asked where she lived. As he drove her home, Tameka still couldn't figure out why he was being so nice to her, but she did know that she was grateful to have him there. Once he parked the car, Craig saw her safely to the front door of her building. He hailed a cab for himself so that he could get home and try to figure out what the hell was going through Monica's head when she decided to run someone down. And although Tameka could not identify the driver and didn't recognize the car, he knew all along that it was Monica.

# CHAPTER THIRTY-THREE

Brook left the hospital and had been staying with Eric ever since. He had refused to let her return to the condo with Tameka. It was his position that since they were less than a month away from their wedding, Brook's moving in now would be no big deal. He just wanted to keep her safe. He even had movers to pack up her belongings and move them out of the condo. He had been unable to convince Brook to kick Tameka out and knew that he ultimately had to respect her final decision.

After Eric got up and took off for the gym, Mia went over to pick Brook up. They had planned to have Tameka meet them at the bridal shop so that they could pick up their gowns and make sure all of the alterations were perfect. Brook was so excited; she was only three days away from becoming a married woman.

Tameka rolled out of bed, showered and got dressed all in preparation to meet Mia and Brook. She now wished that she had nothing to do with this wedding. She knew that the only reason she was still a part of it was because Brook had no time to try and replace her. Her dress had already been ordered and altered and now Brook and Eric were stuck with her.

"Alright, Wayne, I'm out of here. I'll see you later."

"Try to be a little more excited, baby. I know that you don't want to be bothered with this wedding stuff anymore, but just try to be happy and supportive for Brook."

"To hell with being supportive, Wayne. They weren't supportive of me when some maniac almost ran me down. They all turned on me like I threw Brook out in front of the car. No one asked her to save me. I would have at least been able to get a little sympathy and attention for myself if I'd been the one to get hit."

"Well, I'm glad it worked out the way it did. I love you too much to see you hurt or possibly lose you to some idiot with an ax to grind. By the way, have they been able to track down any more leads on who was driving the car?"

"No. I know it was Monica, but there's just no way to prove it."

"Have you seen or heard from her since the incident."

"No, so I'm hoping that she has chilled out. But I've got to get going, baby, see
you later."

"Okay and try to have a little fun."

"Yeah, right."

Tameka left and it wasn't long before she pulled into a parking spot in front of the bridal shop. She waited in her car for Brook and Mia to arrive. It was no more than five minutes before Mia whipped her car into a space. Tameka could see them look over at her and speak a few words.

"Okay Mia, remember you promised to be nice for me. This is a happy time for me, so please be nice to Tameka."

"Only for you, Brook, only for you."

The ladies got out of their cars and Brook immediately gave Tameka a big hug and thanked her for coming. Brook knew that she was being foolish but she couldn't help but feel a little sorry for Tameka. Everyone had turned on her when the reality was that Brook is the one that stepped in front of the car. She was trying to save a friend who was in harm's way. Mia spoke pleasantly to Tameka but no hugs were exchanged.

They made their way into the shop and played dress up. Each one tried on their dress and modeled it for the others. While Mia and Tameka looked gorgeous in their gowns, Brook was absolutely breath taking. Even Tameka let her guard down long enough to express her sincere feelings about how Brook was going to be the most beautiful bride she'd ever seen. Once they were changed and back in their street clothes, Brook suggested they grab some brunch and go over the final details before the rehearsal the next night. Both Mia and Tameka agreed and Tameka followed them to the restaurant.

"I'm so proud of you, Mia. You were respectful and kind to Tameka, even during brunch. I know you don't care for her, but I really do appreciate you for tolerating her for me."

"Brook, you know that I'll do anything for you. You are my best friend and I just want to see you happy."

"Well, I promise you, I never thought I'd have this kind of happiness. I felt that my happiness died with my parents, but then God sent me Eric. He restored my joy and I can't thank Him enough for it."

They pulled up in front of Mia's home and dropped off their gowns. Brook was leaving hers there because that was where she would spend the night tomorrow after the rehearsal dinner. The limo would pick Brook, Mia and Tameka up from Mia's place. Yes, believe it or not, Mia had agreed to let Tameka spend the night with them the night before the wedding and ride to the church together. Mia was truly an exceptional friend.

Tameka returned home and immediately ran to the bathroom. She felt queasy and sick to the stomach. She sat on the toilet for a moment and then jumped up, turned around and threw up in the commode. She had been feeling this way for a couple of weeks and couldn't figure out why. She brushed her teeth, gargled and turned to walk out, but was stopped by Wayne standing in the door way of the bathroom. He had a silly grin on his face and was holding something behind his back.

"Why are you looking at me like that, Wayne? And why are you blocking the door? I want to go and lay down."

"Tameka, you've been feeling like this for a while now, have you stopped to think that maybe you're pregnant?"

"Yeah right," Tameka said with a little laughter in her voice.

"Well, you may think I'm joking, but I'm serious, baby. So I got this while you were out." Wayne pulled an EPT home pregnancy test from a bag he was holding behind him.

"Wayne, you've got to be kidding me."

"Just take it, Tameka; let's find out if I'm going to be a daddy."

Tameka hesitantly took the test from Wayne's hand and closed the bathroom door. She read the directions and urinated on the stick for several seconds. Tameka laid the stick down flat, washed her hands and opened the door. "We have to wait three minutes for the results."

"Okay."

"Wayne, how will you feel if I am pregnant?"

"Baby girl, I will feel great! You know how badly I want children."

"But we're not married yet."

"So, we'll move the wedding date up a few months."

"Are you sure?"

"I'm positive."

"Wayne, I had actually thought that I might be pregnant, but I was not sure how you would feel about it. I'm really relieved to hear that you would be happy."

"Of course I'd be happy, Tameka. I love you and I'm ready for us to be one big happy family."

Tameka stepped back into the bathroom and picked up the stick. There were two pink lines indicating a positive result. She turned slowly and looked at Wayne.

"Well?"

"Well, Daddy, we'd better make an appointment with my ob/gyn."

Wayne scooped up his bride-to-be and kissed her passionately. They giggled and kissed and hugged one another as their hearts filled with more joy than they imagined they could feel.

# CHAPTER THIRTY-FOUR

The rehearsal and dinner that followed went off without a hitch. Everyone was exceptionally nice to one another. Even the girls night at Mia's had been more pleasant and uneventful than Brook had hoped for. The three of them laughed and talked late into the night. Tameka thought about sharing her baby news but decided to let this weekend be all about Brook.

Even after everyone else had gone to bed, Brook had a hard time drifting off to sleep. She couldn't believe how excited and nervous she was. It wasn't an uncomfortable kind of nervous, but more of anticipation as to what the future held for her. Finally around 2:00am sleep took over and Brook found a peaceful rest. She had the most beautiful dream about her parents. They told her how proud they were of her and each one kissed her gently. Then they were gone. When she awoke the next morning, Brook couldn't remember exactly what she dreamed, but there was an uncommonly strong feeling of love that seemed to envelope her.

The limo was waiting outside for Brook, Mia and Tameka, but Brook was still running around inside like a chicken with its head cut off.

"Brook, what are you looking for, honey?" Mia asked.

"My make-up bag, have you seen it?"

"It's in the car with everything else you need."

"Oh, but I can't find the gift I bought for Eric."

"I packed it in your large suitcase last night, remember?" Tameka chimed in.

"Oh yeah."

"Brook, we have everything you need," Mia said with a reassuring hug. "We just need to go before Eric thinks you left him at the altar."

"Okay, let's go."

Eric, David and Eric's cousin, Rick, were already at the church, dressed and waiting. They all lounged leisurely in a small, but comfortable room reserved for the groom and his friends.

"Man, I still say you should have let us given you that bachelor party."

"Rick, man, I didn't need any of that. Looking at a bunch of scantily clad women dance around does nothing for me."

"Yeah, Eric, you need to go on and get married because you are sprung," Rick said with laughter in his voice. "Isn't that right, David?"

"Oh yeah, but I could've told you that a long time ago. This man fell for Brook as soon as he saw her. She has been all he talks about for the longest. But I'm not mad at you, Eric, I know how you feel."

"Then why don't you take that plunge?" Eric asked."

"I will as soon as Mia is ready."

"I hear you man."

The church was now filling up. More of Brook's extended family came down from Maryland than she ever imagined. It touched her to know that they still cared so much about her and wanted to share in her happiness. It was now only fifteen minutes away from show time. Tameka and Mia took these last few minutes to make sure Brook was all together and then Mia presented her with a blue lace garter and Tameka gave her a new satin handkerchief to catch her tears.

"Thank you guys so much. But I can't believe I didn't think about the something borrowed."

"I did," Ms. Williams said as she entered the bridal suite. "Brook, you know I love you like you are my own. This here is a ring my mama gave me before she died. It's very precious to me, but I want you to wear it today as your something borrowed."

"Ms. Williams, it's beautiful. I don't know how to thank you," Brook said while choking back tears.

"You don't have to thank me, it's just a loan. But you stop that crying before you mess up that lovely face of yours. You can't let that man see you with mascara streaked across your face."

All four of them laughed and shared a group hug. Then Toni, the wedding coordinator, entered the room and told them that it was show time.

The music started and the two large doors swung open. First Tameka entered the church and proceeded gracefully down the aisle. Then came Mia looking as beautiful as ever. David's face lit up with a wide grin and Mia's eyes immediately fell on his face. The flower girl came behind Mia dropping soft rose petals as she made her way down the aisle. The little girl looked adorable. The doors closed and the wedding march began to play. All of the guests rose to their feet. The doors re-opened and there stood Brook. She looked like an angel sent straight from the heavens. Brook stood in the doorway for a moment and surveyed the church. The dozens of flowers flown in from everywhere were gorgeous. Her eye's moved across the church as she smiled in acknowledgement of all the people. And then her eye's fell upon the large, beautifully framed picture of her parents at the front of the church. Finally, she looked at Eric and her heart melted. She took a deep breath and made her way down the aisle.

"Can you believe we're married. its official, baby, you are my wife...forever."

Brook leaned in and kissed her husband once more. She could not be happier. The limo made its way through town and the newlywed couple sat in back grinning from ear to ear.

"Okay, we'll have a great time at the reception, but we will end up leaving our guests to party without us. I can't wait to get you alone."

"Well, Mr. Banks, you'll just have to be patient. After all, this is the only wedding reception we'll ever have."

"I know, but I still can't wait to get you alone."

They arrived at the reception hall and waited in a back room for a while to allow time for the guests to arrive. Once the hall was full, Toni came and got the couple and formally introduced them to everyone as Mr. and Mrs. Eric Banks. The couple greeted their guests and the reception kicked into high gear. The food was excellent and after the Best Man and Maid of Honor made their toasts, Brook and Eric headed to the center of the room for their first dance.

Three hours later the party was still going strong. Eric gave Brook a look that let her know it was time for them to make their great escape. They eased away from the party and changed clothes. A few minutes later they returned and thanked their guests and told them to stay and party as long as they wanted. Brook threw the bouquet and guess who caught it…Tameka. She looked back at Wayne and they smiled lovingly at one another. Then Brook and Eric took off for a two week long honeymoon in Hawaii.

# CHAPTER THIRTY-FIVE

"You mean I'm going to be a grandma? Oh, baby, that's fabulous. How far along are you?"

"I'm only eight weeks Mama. Are you really happy for me?"

"Of course I am. The question is, how does Wayne feel about it?"

"Mama, that man is so happy he's about to drive me crazy. All he does is ask me 'what I need, what can I get you, you sure you feel okay?' I don't know if I can take it for seven more months." Tameka said with a smile.

"Girl, just be grateful for the love and attention. And take advantage of it now cause when those seven months are up it'll be all about that baby."

"I hear you, Ma. I have some more news."

"Child, I don't know how much more I can take."

"We've moved the wedding date up. Two months from now I'll be a married woman. And hopefully I won't be showing yet."

"Girl, it won't matter if you're showing or not. I'm so happy for you, Tameka. I'm glad to see your life on this track. It's so much better for you."

"Thanks, Ma, my life is better. I'm so happy."

"Are you hungry? Let me cook for you. What will it be, fish or chicken?"

"Well, if you insist, I'll take the fish."

The mother and daughter talked and ate and laughed at the prospect of Tameka becoming a mom. Tameka was so pleased, so satisfied to know that her mom was really proud of her. Finally, she had done something right.

"So, when are you going to move out of Brooks and in with Wayne?"

"Not until after we're married. I'm going to enjoy my last couple of months of freedom in my own space."

"I understand that, baby."

"I just hope that Brook will let me out of that iron clad lease without a problem. Once she moved out, she had me sign a new lease."

"Well, I understand that she has to protect herself, but why didn't you just move out when she left? You and Wayne were already planning to get married."

"What can I say, Mom, I just love that place. I wasn't ready to give it up. I figured I still had a year before the wedding, so why not enjoy it in luxury."

"I guess."

Tameka spent another thirty minutes with her mom and then left for home. Tomorrow was a work day and she wanted to get plenty of rest. She stopped at the drug store on the way home and was shocked to see Craig in there with Monica, of all people. They looked pretty chummy too and that just really threw Tameka off. She couldn't understand what they were doing together. Craig turned around and saw her staring at them. He just looked at her like he couldn't understand the look of shock on her face. Tameka paid for her merchandise, slowly turned and left the store.

Angrily, Monica looked at Craig, "I wish I could just rip her head off."

"Monica, it's time for you to let it go and move on with your life. You've got a new job, try to focus on that."

"I thought you were on my side."

"I am and that's why you're here with me now instead of in jail. Don't you realize that you could have killed that woman?"

"I never meant to hurt anyone but Tameka. I feel so badly about her friend."

"Then let that feeling keep you from doing something foolish. You're getting everything together now so let's just move forward in a positive direction."

"You're right, besides, Tameka will ultimately pay for all that she's done. I'll just continue to pray for forgiveness for my wrong doings."

"That's my girl."

The next day at work, Tameka made a point to seek out Craig. She wanted to know all the details about the sick little union she saw the night before and wanted Craig to tell her if Monica really was driving the car the day Brook was hit.

"Craig, would you mind stepping into my office for a moment?"

"Sure, I've got a minute. What's up?"

Tameka closed the door behind Craig and sat behind her desk. "What's up with you and Monica? I never realized you two were friends."

"Well, I guess you could say that we're new friends."

"How new?"

"Why, Tameka? Why do you care if me and Monica are friends or not?"

"Just curious I guess. You all never seemed to pay one another any attention when she worked here."

"Look, we recently bumped into one another and have been enjoying each other company on a consistent basis. Now, if you'll excuse me, I have work to do."

"Craig, one more thing, is she the one that tried to run me down?"

"Get a grip, Tameka, she's not the only one you've ever offended."

With that, Craig left her office and Tameka still didn't have the answer she really wanted. She should have known that he would never tell her the truth. Even if he knew who was to blame. Tameka took a deep breath and decided to move on with her day and her life. She wouldn't give the mystery driver any more of her time or worry. She now had bigger fish to fry. She had a wedding to plan and a baby to nurture. Her concentration would now be on making a new life for herself and loving her man and her baby. Her very own baby, something that even Brook didn't have right now. Someone that would always love and accept her no matter what.

# CHAPTER THIRTY-SIX

Mia picked up the rest of the treats she and David had planned to leave for the newlyweds. She only had thirty minutes until she was supposed to meet David at Eric and Brook's home. They thought it would be nice to fill the fridge with food and leave fresh flowers and balloons to welcome them home.

Mia pulled into the drive right behind David. They greeted each other with hugs and kisses. Kisses that were getting a little too passionate for the driveway of a friend's house. There was a mom jogging behind a baby stroller that obviously thought that their behavior was completely inappropriate. Mia found much humor in the mom's reaction. She and David gathered the packages and made their way into the house.

"So how long have you had a key to Eric's house?"

"Ever since he bought it. He has one to mine also, just for security reasons. You should have at least one person that has a key to your place, you know in case you get locked out or leave town and need someone to check on things."

"Yes dear, I know. Brook has always had a key to my home. Now, let's get this stuff put up so we can get out of here."

"And what are we going to do when we leave?"

"What did you have in mind?"

"You know what I have in mind."

"David, you are such a pervert."

"And you love it."

"Yes, I do, but how about we go grab some lunch instead. Save that other stuff for later."

"If you insist."

Mia gave David a little peck on the cheek and went about the business of putting the food away and arranging the flowers and balloons. It wasn't long before they were heading into town for lunch.

A short time later the taxi pulled in front of the house and Eric and Brook stepped out. The driver took their bags to the door and Eric paid the man. Then he unlocked the door and swooped his bride up and carried her over the threshold. This tickled Brook so much. She was laughing uncontrollably and trying to kiss on Eric at the same time. Once he put her down and brought the luggage inside they were pleased beyond words to see what Mia and David had done. Everything was beautiful and the card they left was so sweet.

"We are so lucky to have such good friends."

"Yes, baby, we are, but even luckier to have each other."

"You say the sweetest things. Promise me that you'll never change. Promise me Eric that you'll always be this loving and attentive."

"You know I will. How could I not always love someone like you?"

"You're the best, babe. And now all this sugary sweet talk is starting to sound a little goofy. Are you hungry?"

"Oh yeah, I'm starving. What do you want?"

"Let's go to that little Thai restaurant."

"Alright, let's go."

As the hostess led Brook and Eric to their table, they were surprised to see David and Mia sitting across the room. They made their way to the other side of the restaurant and surprised their friends. "Hey ya'll," Brook said cheerfully.

"Brook, hey girl. How long have you guys been here?" Mia asked as she gave Brook and Eric both a warm and loving hug.

"We just got back. We dropped our things off at the house and headed over here. And thank you guys so much for the food and flowers and balloons. That was a great way to welcome us home."

"It was our pleasure."

"Eric, man, our food hasn't come out yet, why don't you two join us at our table?" David asked.

"Cool with us."

Before they realized it, the group of friends had been sitting and talking for almost two hours. The food was long gone but, the conversation just kept flowing. Finally Eric said it was time for them go. He paid the check and they all walked out together. As they walked out the door and started to head down the flight of stairs, they were greeted by Tameka and Wayne. Tameka was a little winded from the climb up the stairs.

"Hey everybody, when did you two get back?" Tameka asked while hugging Brook.

"We just got in a few hours ago. How are you guys doing?"

"We are great." Tameka said with a huge smile. "As a matter of fact, we have some great news to share. I'm pregnant!"

"Oh my gosh, congratulations," Brook squealed.

Everyone congratulated the two and even Mia seemed genuinely happy for them. It was nice to see Tameka so happy for herself instead of being jealous of someone else. Tameka went on to tell them all about the new wedding date and how the ceremony would now be scaled back a little because of the time crunch. They shared a little more small talk and said their good-byes. But when Tameka turned to go in the door, the heel of her shoe got caught in a crack of the cement step. She lost her balance and tumbled down the entire flight of stairs. Despite his efforts, Wayne was unable to stop her fall.

Mia dialed 911 as everyone else ran down the steps to Tameka. Brook told her not to move and held her friends head in her lap. Brook tried her best to comfort Tameka and reassure her that everything would be okay. The guys tried their best to keep Wayne calm so that he didn't further upset Tameka. The ambulance arrived and the EMS workers asked what happened. Brook explained the situation and they asked Tameka questions about how she felt and what her pain level was. They then braced her neck and placed her on a stretcher. Mia glared at Brook with a look of horror when she saw the blood stain that Tameka left on the ground.

On the way to the hospital, Brook called Ms. Williams to inform her of everything that had happened. Ms. Williams immediately left home and met them all at the hospital. It seemed as if they waited for hours for someone to come and give them an update on Tameka's condition. Unfortunately, the look on the doctor's face did not look very promising. He advised them that Tameka would be okay. She had several bad bruises, but worse of all, the fall had caused damage to the fetus and the pregnancy was spontaneously aborted.

Ms. Williams wept out loud. Her heart hurt so badly for her little girl. Wayne tried to get himself together so that he could go back and try to be of some comfort to his woman. A few moments passed and Wayne left the waiting area for Tameka's room. As soon as he stepped in the door, Tameka burst into tears.

"Oh God, Wayne, I lost the baby, I lost my baby!"

"I know, baby, I know. But it'll be okay. I promise that it will be okay."

"How can you say that? The thing I wanted most is gone."

"Tameka, I wanted the baby too. But please remember that we still have each other and we can try again. You'll get pregnant again."

"But it won't be this baby, this baby is gone forever."

"Yes, he is and as hard as it is, we have to accept that this was God's will."

"Get out."

"What?"

"Get out, Wayne. Get the hell out of my room!"

Wayne returned to the waiting area with tears in his eyes. He was hurt that he'd just lost his child and hurt that he was unable to comfort the woman he loved. He was unable to be what she needed right now and that hurt him deeply. He took a seat and Brook went to him and gave him her shoulder to lean on and a comforting word and touch to help ease his pain. At the same time, Ms. Williams left the waiting area to go and be with her baby.

Ms. Williams entered the room and didn't say a word. She went to Tameka and held her in her arms. The mother and daughter cried together and it was exactly what Tameka needed. Someone to hold her and feel her pain.

# CHAPTER THIRTY-SEVEN

It had been two months since Tameka lost her baby. Since then she had moved the wedding date back to what it was originally supposed to be and decided to continue to live in the condo. All of this was contrary to what Wayne wanted. But what he wanted didn't really seem to matter much. The kinder and gentler Tameka that was present while she was pregnant was now gone and the old Tameka was back with a vengeance. She didn't give a crap about anyone, but herself. As far as she was concerned, she had been robbed of her only real joy and didn't feel the need to try and make anyone else happy.

Ms. Williams had been warning Tameka that while Wayne loved her, he wouldn't hang around and take her abuse forever. No man could take the way that she had been treating him, so cold and distant, as if everything was his fault.

"Baby, he loved and wanted that child just as much as you did. Why don't you share your pain with him? Y'all can be of comfort to each other instead of turning against him."

"Maybe he can't comfort me. He will never understand how I feel."

"No, he won't, because he's a man. He thinks differently and feels differently from you, but it doesn't mean that he don't feel hurt and pain. He's the best thing that ever happened to you and you are going to ruin the relationship. If you get it together, the two of you could go on to have a litter of babies and be happy together for years to come."

"Mama please, I may never be able to have a child. I might not ever be able to get pregnant again."

"Why not? I got pregnant with you after I lost my baby."

"You never told me that."

"Didn't see the point until now. My point is that you can go on to have a lot of babies and be completely happy if you start acting like you got the sense God gave you. You are not the only woman to ever lose a child. It happens every day Tameka."

"But not to me."

"So, you're going to let this change you into an uglier person than you were before you ever got pregnant. How was that working out for you?"

"It was working just fine, thank you."

"So fine that someone tried to run you down and almost killed the only real friend you've ever had.

"I'm out of here."

"The truth hurts, doesn't it?"

"Bye, Mama."

"Bye."

Tameka took off and headed towards Brooks. She was supposed to be picking Brook and Mia up for a day of shopping. She already knew that she didn't want to be bothered with Mia any more than Mia wanted to be bothered with her. They were only hanging out with her to try and cheer her up. But hell, it had been two months and Tameka was as cheered up as she was going to get. She just wanted everything to get back to normal. She wanted Wayne to stop pestering her, she wanted she and Mia to go back to their dislike of each other and wanted her mom to get off of her case. They all needed to realize that Tameka was fine. She liked who she was and the way she behaved. It was other folks with the problem.

As soon as she pulled into the drive, Mia and Brook came skipping out like two silly school girls. Tameka felt like she could throw up on the spot. She started to just punch the gas and leave their ass's in the drive way. Instead, she put a grin on her face and played their little happy game.

"Hi ladies, are you both ready to shop till you drop?"

"Hey, Tameka," Brook said as she slid in the front seat. "We are ready to go."

"Yes we are," Chimed in Mia.

"Well, I figured we could hit Lenox first and then maybe go across the street to Phipps Plaza. What do ya'll think?"

"Sounds like a plan. Later tonight Mia and David are coming over for a little cook out, why don't you and Wayne join us?"

"I'll call him a little later and see if he's up for it."

Tameka knew the moment the invitation crossed Brook's lips that she would not be in attendance. There was no way she was going to subject herself to being surrounded by that bunch of unrealistically happy go lucky folks. She just couldn't stomach it. She continued to drive and listened to them chatter away and she added a word here or there just to make it seem as if she cared about what they were discussing.

They walked the mall and stopped in almost every store. Each of them did their fair share of spending and this was something that Tameka actually enjoyed. She loved treating herself to nice things. She felt that she deserved to be able to dress well and look good at all times. Besides, she was a public figure now. She had to look good. As they continued on through the mall, Tameka wondered to herself why Brook seemed to slow as they approached the different maternity shops. But then she realized that it was all in her head, she realized that maybe it was actually her slowing down to take a look at what was no longer a part of her life.

After spending about three hours shopping, they all decided it was time for lunch. There was no way that Brook could go without eating until the barbeque that night. They all agreed on Italian and headed for the restaurant. It wasn't long before they were enjoying a delicious meal and sharing conversation that covered an array of topics.

"So, Tameka, are you going to call Wayne and see if he wants to join us tonight?" Brook asked.

"No, I'm kind of tired and think that I'm just going to take it easy and get a little rest tonight. The job has been wearing me out."

"I hear you, but I do wish you would reconsider."

"I know, but just please accept my apologies. I am tired."

"Alright, I'll leave you alone and stop asking. But I do have something that I need to tell you. I'm not quite sure how I'm supposed to share this with you, but you'll eventually figure it out."

"Okay, you've got me worried. What is it, Brook, just tell me."

"Um…I'm pregnant."

Everything was silent for a moment. Tameka couldn't believe her ears, couldn't believe that Brook was now carrying the baby that should have been hers. This was unreal, it was too much to digest. Tameka just sat there and then something in her mind snapped her back to reality.

"Brook, that is wonderful. You're going to be a mom," Tameka managed to squeak out while giving Brook a big hug. "How far along are you?"

"Right at two months. It appears it happened right after we got back from the honeymoon."

"It appears that the honeymoon never ended," added Mia with a little snicker.

"I guess you're right. You two love birds are going to have to find a bigger nest soon."

"Well, since you've brought it up, me and Eric are in the process of meeting with our builder to finalize plans for the new house we're having built."

"Well, damn, you're just full of good news. Mama will be so happy for you."

"I know, I can't wait to tell Ms. Williams."

"Well, ladies, I am tired. Are you all ready to go?"

"Sure, Tameka. I've got to start preparing for tonight anyway."

They paid the check and left for home. Tameka was very quiet on the ride to Brooks house and her silence didn't go unnoticed. Both Brook and Mia tried several times to get her to participate in various conversations, but she just shrugged them off and excused herself from conversation by blaming her exhaustion. Once she pulled in front of the house, Tameka gave both Mia and Brook a light pat on the back and a pleasant good-bye. She pulled off before the doors were even closed good.

Wayne came over shortly after Tameka got home. He could tell immediately that something was terribly wrong. The condo was a mess; it looked as if a tornado had come through. Tameka's face was streaked with mascara where she had obviously been crying. Her hair looked as if she'd tried to pull it out strand by strand.

"Baby, what happened? What's wrong?"

"She's got my baby, Wayne. The bitch that has everything now has my baby."

"Okay, Tameka, I'm lost. Who has your baby?"

"Brook! The heffa is pregnant. I'm the one who's supposed to be having the baby. That was the one thing that I was going to have before her. The one thing that she wouldn't beat me at and now she's pregnant."

She actually had Wayne scared. He didn't know what to make of her behavior. He was truly afraid of what she might do.

"Tameka, you are not in competition with Brook. You are your own person and shouldn't allow yourself to be affected by anything that she does. You are more successful career wise than she'll ever be."

"She doesn't have to be successful career wise, Wayne, she's rich as cream. She lives the kind of life that little girls dream about. Did you know that she and Eric are having a fucking mansion built? What does she care about a career?"

Wayne held Tameka while she sobbed. He was so confused as to how to handle or comfort her. He had never seen anyone so obsessed with someone else's life. He could not understand why she couldn't be happy with the life that she had made for herself. Couldn't understand why she couldn't be happy with the life that they could build together. And as he held her, Tameka came to the realization that he didn't know and would never understand her. She would never be able to get him to see things from her point of view. So she decided to dry up and let him believe that he'd helped her feel better and that her little tantrum was over. She would keep her feelings to herself from now own.

"Tameka, I promise you that together we will make a great life for ourselves. We will have our own family and a beautiful home. You'll be proud of the life we make together. I promise."

"I know, baby, I guess I just had to get all of this off of my chest. Jealousy is an ugly thing and I hate that I let it do this to me," Tameka said with an ugly smirk on her face.

She didn't mean a word of what she was saying and Wayne should have realized that. But instead he chose to believe what made him feel better about his beloved Tameka. He would soon learn to see her for what she was and not the woman he wanted her to be. But for now, he held her in his arms and held on to the dream that he had of the wonderful life he wanted them to share.

Meanwhile, across town, Brook, Eric, Mia and Dave raised their soda glasses in a toast to celebrate the pregnancy. Brook was thrilled to be sharing this happy time in their life with their closest friends. She was sorry that Tameka couldn't share in her happiness, but she realized from the beginning that this would be a hard pill for Tameka to swallow. After all, she had just lost her child and Brook could definitely sympathize with that.

"What are you thinking about, baby? You got quiet on us," Eric asked.

"Oh, pay me no attention. I wasn't thinking about anything."

Mia looked at her suspiciously, "I bet she was thinking about Tameka and her reaction to the news."

"What was her reaction?" Eric asked curiously.

"It was fake happiness and then she couldn't get away from us fast enough," Mia chimed.

"Well, Mia, you know she just lost her own baby. Cut her some slack."

"Brook, heed my warning, cutting Tameka slack is ultimately going to cause you grief. The girl has never wanted anything good for you. We all know it and that's why we try to watch your back as far as she is concerned. But trust your best friend when I tell you that you better watch your own back around her."

# CHAPTER THIRTY-EIGHT

Tameka managed to get Wayne up and out of her house before the break of day. She had a busy day ahead of her and wanted to get an early start. She arrived at work early to tie up some loose ends she had left the previous week. She went over copy for the noon news and patiently waited for her producer so that they could firm up the final stories. She'd already spoken with the station manager and gotten permission to cut out as soon as the broadcast was over. She had an afternoon appointment that she could not miss.

The broadcast went off without a hitch and Tameka couldn't have been happier. She ran right out of the station, jumped in her car and was now pulling up in front of a family planning clinic. She prepared herself to give a great performance to whatever doctor was on staff.

"How may I help you?"

"Hi, I'm Miss Williams, I called earlier for an urgent appointment."

"Yes, Miss Williams, I'm delighted to meet you. I actually have to say that I'm a fan," the geeky looking woman said with a foolish grin.

"Oh thank you, but I'd really like to stay anonymous."

"Of course, Miss Williams, your privacy will be greatly respected. Please fill out this information and we will be with you shortly."

"Thank you very much."

Tameka sat down with the clip board and aside from her name filled it out fraudulently. Everything on the paper was a lie and everything that she would tell the doctor would be a lie as well. But hey, a girls gotta do what a girls gotta do.

"Miss Williams," called a tall, skinny nurse, "the doctor will see you now."

Tameka stood up and looked around the room once more. She was thankful that no one else seemed to have noticed her. She grabbed her bag and followed the nurse to an exam room. Tameka was given a paper gown and asked to undress completely and drape herself in the gown. She advised the nurse that she knew exactly what she needed and an exam was not it. But if she wanted their help she had no choice. So she did as she was told and put on the paper gown. It wasn't long before the doctor entered the room.

"Hello, Miss Williams, I'm Dr. Ashley Biggs. What brings you in today?

"Well doctor, I had an unwanted sexual encounter last night and I'm afraid that it may result in pregnancy. I want to make sure that that doesn't happen."

"Are you telling me that you were raped?"

"I guess it is what's referred to as a date rape. I was out with what I thought was a nice gentleman. We went back to my place for a drink and he forced himself on me."

"I am so sorry, Miss Williams. This is the most common form of rape. Have you notified the police?"

"No, I can't. I am somewhat of a public figure and I don't want to become a news story. I want to just keep it private and take care of any unforeseen problems."

"I understand your position, but I would still urge you to try and press charges."

"I'm sorry, I just can't."

"I understand. Well, let's examine you. I will run a series of tests to make sure that you did not contract a STD including an AIDS test. Are you on birth control?"

"No, I'm not and that is my greatest concern right now."

"Well, I'm sure you've heard of the Morning After pill. I will give you that to take as a precautionary measure."

"How effective is the pill?"

"Very, it will definitely insure that you are not pregnant as a result of this unfortunate incident. Let's get on with it, shall we."

Dr. Biggs found just what Tameka knew she would, Wayne's sperm from the night before and the normal abrasions that come from a night of rough sex. Therefore, the doctor had no problem believing her little sick story. The doctor left the room and Tameka got dressed and patiently waited for her to return. It wasn't long before the door swung open and Dr. Biggs walked back in.

"Alright, Miss Williams, the office will notify you with the results of your tests and here is a package with the Morning After pill we discussed. You'll want to take it right away."

"May I please have a second package?"

"Miss Williams, one is all you need. It should take care of everything."

"Please, just for my peace of mind..." Tameka said through her fake sobs and tears. "I've never experienced anything like this before and I need to be sure. I can't allow myself to carry that bastard's child. The thought of it makes me ill. Please give me another package, please?" Tameka broke down in an uncontrollable mess of sobs.

"I promise that the one package will do, but if it will give you peace of mind, I guess I don't see the harm." Dr. Biggs replied very reluctantly.

Tameka laughed and patted herself on the back all the way to the baby store. She was so impressed with her acting skills that for a moment she thought she might be in the wrong business. She parked her car and entered the store behind a big pregnant lady and her husband. Tameka found the prettiest and most expensive layette that they had. She purchased it and headed back to the car. On her way home she called Brook and asked her to please stop by the condo on her way home from work. Brook reluctantly agreed, said she guessed it would be okay since Eric had to work late anyway. Tameka thanked her and hit the end button on her phone. She couldn't be happier.

Tameka got home and relaxed for a while. She laid on the sofa and watched Oprah, something she seldom got to do. Around 5:00 she got up, straightened up her mess and went into the kitchen to put on some baked chicken, rice and green beans. Brook had always loved the marinade she used to cook her chicken. Tameka even made a nice pitcher of decaffeinated ice tea; she knew how much Brook loved tea. It was about an hour later that the doorbell rang. Tameka put a smile on her face and went to open the door.

"Hi, Brook, thank you so much for coming over."

"Not a problem, what's up?"

"Well, come on in to the kitchen and I'll tell you."

They made their way into the kitchen and Brook couldn't help but take in the aroma of the food Tameka had prepared. She even noticed the beautifully wrapped gift box on the table.

"Your dinner smells good, Wayne must be coming over?"

"Actually, I made it for us. I was hoping that you'd stay and eat with me."

"That was awfully nice of you. I have to say I'm surprised. You seemed less than enthused to be around me Saturday."

"Yes, that's why I wanted you to come by. Brook, I owe you an apology. When you told me that you were pregnant it just kind of threw me. I will admit that my immediate reaction was jealousy. But I've come to realize that I don't need to rain on your parade. You were happy and supportive of me and I need to be the same for you."

"It's okay, Tameka. I can understand how you could be a little upset."

"But I had no right to act so ugly. I know that my time will come around again. But for now I'll be happy to be an auntie to your precious little baby. And on that note, I want to give you your first baby gift." Tameka reached over and handed Brook the gift box.

"Oh my goodness, Tameka, it's gorgeous. I don't even know what to say. This is really a gorgeous layette. Thank you so much."

"You are welcome. So how about dinner? I even made ice tea, decaffeinated of course."

"I'd love to stay for dinner."

"Well, I'll fix our plates while you go wash up."

Brook went to the restroom to clean up for dinner and while she was gone Tameka got busy. Before she fixed their plates she put some ice into a couple glasses and poured up some tea. She pulled out the packages of pills that Dr. Biggs had given her and crushed them up. Tameka poured every bit of the crushed pills into Brook's glass. When Brook came back into the kitchen, Tameka handed her the glass of tea and Brook took a seat at the table. Tameka then sat a plate of food in front of Brook and sat a plate on the table for herself. The two friends laughed and talked and ate until they were full enough to burst. Brook hadn't realized how late it was getting until Eric called on her cell phone.

"Tameka, thank you for everything. Dinner was great and I love the gift you gave me for the baby. It means a lot to me to know that I have your support in this."

"Girl, you've got all my support. Anything I can do for you and my niece or nephew, I will."

"Well, I have to go, but thanks again."

"Any time, be careful and have a good night."

"You too."

The two hugged and Brook left for home. Tameka had never been so pleased with herself. She took comfort in the fact that Brook would now know what it was really like to lose something she wanted so badly. It was time Brook took a walk in her shoes.

# CHAPTER THIRTY-NINE

It wasn't long before Brook arrived home and was greeted at the door by Eric. They went inside and Brook couldn't wait to show him the baby gift she had received. She went on to tell Eric about Tameka's apology and the wonderful dinner she prepared for them to share.

"So, baby, do you think that she was really sincere or just setting you up for something later?"

"No, she was sincere. She meant everything she said. And just look at this layette, she spent plenty of money on this."

"I just find it hard to believe that Tameka could really be sincere and apologetic about anything."

"Don't be so hard on her, Eric. Somewhere deep down inside she has a good heart and every now and then it comes shining through."

"Yeah right, I'll make a deal with you. I won't be so hard on her if you are more cautious of her."

"Yeah, yeah. What did you have for dinner, do you want me to fix you something?"

""No, we ordered in Chinese at the office."

"Okay. Well I'm going to go take a shower and put on my P.J's so I can relax."

Brook headed to the bedroom and it wasn't long before she was dressed for bed. She picked up a novel she had been reading and propped herself up in the bed to try and finish it. Nothing relaxed her like a good book. But for some reason she couldn't get comfortable. She was feeling a little nauseous and uneasy. Eric walked into the room and watched her as he prepared to take his shower.

"Are you okay, baby? You look a little funny."

"Yes, I guess I'm okay, just feeling a little queasy."

"Maybe it's morning sickness or in this case, night sickness. Didn't the doctor say that you could get it at any time during the day?"

"Yes she did, but would that explain why my stomach feels like this?"

"How does it feel?"

"Kind of griping. You know how you feel when you take a laxative that has trouble working."

"Do you think we should call the doctor?"

"No, I'm sure it will pass. She said I could feel a little discomfort. It should only be a problem if my stomach is cramping and it's not. I think I'll just lie down and go to sleep."

"Alright, baby, I'm going to take a quick shower. I'll be right back and lay down with you."

Brook snuggled up close to her husband and drifted off to sleep. She was having the sweetest dream when she suddenly felt a sharp pain. Brook sat straight up in the bed and grabbed her stomach. The pain went right away, but came back sharper and more intense a minute later. This time the pain didn't let up, Brook was doubled over and crying when Eric woke up and realized that she was in trouble. He turned over to grab the phone and noticed that the bedside clock said 3:28am. Eric dialed the obstetrician's number and got the answering service. They took a message for the doctor and she called back within five minutes. Eric explained what was going on and was told to get Brook to the emergency room right away.

"What did she say?" Brook asked through the tears and moans.

"Come on baby, I have to get you to the emergency room."

Eric threw on some sweats and tennis shoes and picked up his wife and carried her out to the car. He took off down the street with no concern for the speed limit. Within fifteen minutes they were in the hospital parking lot. He picked Brook up and ran with her through the emergency room doors. He was glad to see her physician running in right behind him. They got Brook into a wheel chair and took off with her to the back. But before he could join her, he had to provide insurance and other personal information. Eric basically threw the information at them and took off to the back in search of his wife.

"What's wrong, Dr. Reid?" Eric asked as he burst into the room.

"We are going to do an ultrasound right now, Mr. Banks, to make sure that the baby isn't in distress."

"But doesn't the fact that I'm passing blood already mean that my baby is in trouble?" Brook sobbed.

"It is a strong indication, but we need to know to what extent."

Brook was crying and suffering in severe pain while Dr. Reid performed the ultrasound. Another lab technician was drawing blood for a series of tests. The lab tech left, but Dr. Reid continued with her work. However, the look on her face wasn't one of promise and hope.

"What's wrong, Dr. Reid?" Brook was almost hysterical.

"I'm so sorry, Mr. And Mrs. Banks, but there is no heart beat. I'm unable to detect a heartbeat. The fetus is no longer viable."

Brook was unable to contain her emotions. She broke down crying in her husband's arms and while he was trying to be strong for his wife, his heart was also breaking. He was so ready to be a father. He didn't even bother to try and wipe the tears from his face. He just continued to hold Brook while she sobbed deeply and asked God why.

"Mrs. Banks, we have got to remove the fetus. You would be in unbearable pain if I allowed you to just lay here and do it alone. Let me help you pass it. I'll need for you to lie back please."

Brook was given a sedative and was kept for twenty-four hour observation. Naturally, Eric stayed with her and around 7:00am called Mia so that she could also lend Brook her support. Mia was so upset and told Eric that she'd be there within the hour. It only took Mia thirty minutes to arrive, but on her way she called Tameka and that would prove to be a big mistake.

Mia opened the hospital room door slowly and immediately saw Brook sleeping in the bed. She looked to the corner and saw Eric. He waved for her to come on in. She closed the door and walked further into the room. Mia eased her way over to Eric and gave him a big hug. She took a seat beside him and sat in silence for a few minutes. Then she couldn't go a second longer without asking what went wrong.

"Mia, I don't even know. One minute she said she felt nauseous and was going to sleep. The next thing I know, it's three something in the morning and she's doubled over in pain. The doctor said that these things just happen sometimes and there's not always a reasonable explanation."

"Well, did she have any complaints before this?"

"No, everything was fine. She went to Tameka's place for dinner, came home and took a shower. She had been fine."

Brook slowly woke up and saw Mia and Eric talking. When she attempted to sit up, Mia jumped up to help her. Mia actually ended up sitting on the bed and holding her friend. She just wanted to comfort the two of them. She couldn't imagine their pain and hated to see them having to endure something like this. A moment later the door opened and in walked Dr. Reid.

"Good morning, everyone. How are you feeling, Mrs. Banks?"

"A little groggy, but okay I guess."

"Well I've got a couple of questions to ask you, may I ask you two to step outside?"

"Why can't they stay?" Brook asked with a puzzled look on her face.

"I'm not sure that you would want them to hear everything I have to ask."

"Well, I have no secrets, Dr. Reid. Please just ask or say what you have to say."

"Okay then, Mrs. Banks, are you sure that you didn't have second thoughts about having the baby?"

"I'm positive; I wanted our baby more than anything. Why would you ask me something like that?"

"Your lab work found that there was a high level of a drug commonly used to prevent pregnancy. Have you ever heard of the Morning After pill?"

"Yes, isn't it used to prevent pregnancy after unprotected sex?"

"Yes ma'am, it is and there was double the normal dosage in your blood stream. That coupled with the aspirin was too much for the fetus."

"I don't understand, I haven't taken anything other than my prenatal pills." Brook broke down again in uncontrollable sobs.

"I'm so sorry, Mrs. Banks, I can't offer you any more explanation than that. I certainly can't explain how those drugs got into your system, but I am so very sorry for your loss."

The doctor left the room and as she walked out Tameka walked in. Brook continued to sob while Eric stared Tameka down like she was evil personified. Before Brook even realized that Tameka was in the room, she heard her husband shouting.

"What the fuck did you do to my wife? What did you give her? I know it was you, you sick little bitch!"

"What are you talking about Eric? Mia called and said that

something horrible had happened to Brook, so I came right over."

Without another word, Eric ran across the room and grabbed her by the throat. It was his intention to choke the life right out of her. Mia ran over and tried to pull him away, but he had a death grip on Tameka. It wasn't until he heard Brook begging for him to release her that he let Tameka go. Tameka fell to the floor like a sack of potatoes. She was holding her neck and gasping for air. Mia tried to help her to her feet, but Tameka snatched away from her.

"I should have your ass arrested for assault."

"And we should have you arrested for the murder of our child. What in the hell did you give Brook last night?"

"I just tried to be nice and fix her a nice dinner, Eric!"

"And you laced it with abortion pills, didn't you?"

Brook sat in the middle of the hospital bed in a state of shock. She couldn't believe what she was hearing.

"Tameka, please tell me you didn't do this to me. Please tell me that you wouldn't take my baby from me."

Tameka fixed her hair and clothes, picked up her purse and looked Brook right in the eye. "You should be careful where you eat from now on." Tameka then turned and ran from the room.

# CHAPTER FORTY

It had been two weeks since Brook lost her child and she still hadn't been able to get herself together. She had been sitting at home drowning in a mix of self-pity and anger. She still couldn't believe that Tameka had done this to her and couldn't understand why the police refused to arrest her. The way Brook saw it, Tameka had confessed to them in the hospital so the police didn't need any more evidence than that. As Brook continued to wallow on the couch and look at meaningless television, she heard the doorbell ring. Brook didn't move. The bell rang again and again and still Brook didn't move. Finally, she heard someone come through the front door and call her name. She had known all along that it was Mia.

"Why didn't you open the door?"

"I figured it was you and knew that you'd eventually let yourself in. Why aren't you at work?"

"I left early. Why aren't you up and dressed?"

"Don't want to be."

"So, Brook, you're just going to curl up in a little ball and hide from the world?"

"Sounds like a plan to me."

"What happened to the strong Brook I used to know? You know the sweet girl with the strong survival instinct."

"Mia, I'm tired of being strong. I'm tired of losing the people that are most important to me. Hell, Mia, I'm just tired."

"Well, Eric is still here and I know how important he is to you. It is very difficult for him to see you like this. He is hurting too and wants for you two to get through this together. But you are shutting him out."

"Well I'm sorry, Mia, I just don't have the energy to help him cope. I can barely cope myself. And I have no idea how to pull myself out of this. I thought I'd be better once they arrested that bitch, but the police say that they can't. Little Ms. Tameka gets off scot free."

"Only if you let her. Brook, I know that if we think hard enough we can find a way to pull up some dirt on her. I know that we can think of a way to hurt her the same way she has hurt so many others."

"Mia, we have nothing to hurt her with. I am not even trying to make her suffer. I just wanted her to be held accountable for what she did to me. I wanted someone to make her understand that she killed my baby. It wasn't some inanimate object that she just got rid of. It was a baby, my baby. He had a heart beat and she caused his heart to stop beating. She ripped life right out of my body."

Mia didn't know what to say. All she could do was sit there and hold her friend while that friend, her best friend, tried to cleanse her heart and soul with tears. Several minutes passed and Mia continued to hold Brook in her arms. Thinking out loud, Mia said "all the crap that she has done, someone should've been recording her life for proof of her evilness." Brook didn't immediately respond. She just sat up in silence and then jumped up off the couch. She headed towards her bedroom without saying a word.

"Where are you going?" Mia asked with a confused look on her face.

"Will you take me to the bank?"

"Sure, Brook."

Within minutes, Brook came back into the family room fully dressed and ready to go. They jumped into Mia's car and went straight downtown to Brook's bank. Mia waited in the car while Brook handled her business.

"Hello, how may I help you today?" A customer service representative asked politely.

"Yes, my name is Brook Mansfield-Banks and I need to get into my safety deposit box, please."

Brook presented her identification and her box key and was escorted into the room that held all of the boxes. The woman gave her a minute of privacy and that was all Brook needed to retrieve what she was after. Brook was only in the bank a total of about eight minutes and then ran back out and jumped into the car.

"Let's get back to the house, Mia, I've got something here I want us to see."

On the way back to the house, Brook pulled out her cell phone and called an old friend. She gave him her home address and asked him to please meet her there as soon as possible. Without hesitation he agreed. Brook and Mia were not back at the house ten minutes before the doorbell rang.

"Rodney, it is so good to see you." Brook greeted her old friend with a big hug and a warm smile. "Please come on in."

Rodney followed Brook into the family room and smiled again when he saw Mia sitting on the couch.

"Rodney, oh my goodness it is so good to see you again. Brook, I didn't know that this is who we were waiting for."

"Yes girl, I told you that Rodney is a detective now with the Atlanta Police Department."

"Oh yes. So how are you Rodney, what's been going on?"

"Nothing much, baby girl, just working hard trying to keep the city safe for ya'll."

"Can I get either of you anything to drink before we sit down for our little movie?"

Both Rodney and Mia looked at Brook with puzzled expressions on their faces. What movie could she be talking about? Mia was under the impression that they were hatching a scheme to get Tameka back, not enjoying a matinee. She could have stayed at work if she had known that all Brook wanted was company for a movie.

"Brook sweetheart, I don't really have time to take in a movie. You know duty calls, crimes are being committed as we speak."

"Just cool you're heels, it's not that kind of movie. Rodney, you gave me this years ago and I think it's time we see just what's on it."

Brook put the tape in and sat down. None of them could believe their eyes. It was a tape of Tameka making out with some guy. But just as the guy tried to take it further and get Tameka out of her clothes, she started pushing him away. Whoever he was, he wasn't giving up easily and Tameka seemed to have been getting angrier and angrier. She jumped to her feet and the guy grabbed her by the arm to pull her back down. Tameka grabbed a glass and smashed it against the guys head. He grabbed his head and pulled back a hand full of blood. The guy didn't hesitate to jump up and slap the hell out of Tameka. Then as he headed to the door to apparently kick her out, she grabbed a beer bottle and broke it on the table. Tameka ran up behind him and jabbed the broken bottle into his back. The poor guy fell to the floor and damn if Tameka didn't force the bottle into his neck. Then the tape stopped.

The three of them looked at one another in shock. Their mouths were hung open and no one was able to speak a word for what seemed like an eternity. Finally, Rodney broke the silence.

"Brook, are you sure I gave you that?"

"Yes. Remember my junior year when you went to pick Tameka up for me from that guy's house?"

"Oh my goodness, I forgot about that. I know when I got there I helped Tameka get her stuff and I saw the light blinking on the VCR. I assumed the guy had taped himself raping Tameka and that's why I took the tape. On the way back to campus I stopped at a pay phone and called 911 for the man. I just put it out of my mind after that."

"Well do you have any way of finding out if he really died or not? I remember her telling me his name was Titus and you know where he lived."

"Yeah, I can do a search in our system and find out."

"What made you think that he was recording himself raping Tameka? He didn't rape her." Mia asked, still in a state of shock.

"Well, we know that now, but then Tameka told both of us that he raped her. She had said she killed him. Until you tell me differently Rodney, I'm going to assume that he did die."

Three hours passed and Book and Mia were still at the house waiting to hear back from Rodney. They couldn't believe the things that Tameka was capable of. They talked about all the horrible things she'd done and it hurt Brook to her heart to know that she helped cover up the death of an innocent man. But now, she was determined to get justice for him and revenge for herself. It was time for Tameka to pay.

The phone rang and Brook was relieved to hear Rodney's voice. She didn't know how much longer she could wait for news about Titus.

"He's dead. His death is actually listed as a cold case. She did kill him, paramedics found him dead in his house that night she was picked up. So what do you plan to do with this now, Brook?"

"Well, Rodney, I'm going to the police with the tape. I'll let them know that I was going through some things in the condo where I've allowed Tameka to stay and I found the tape in a box full of other junk. She should find better hiding places."

# CHAPTER FORTY-ONE

Tameka arrived at the station a little early. She wanted to get in and get some coffee and have a moment of quiet time in her office before starting her day. But as soon as she stepped off the elevator, she saw two men dressed in suites and three armed police officers standing with the station manager. They all turned and looked at her and her stomach sank. Tameka had a very uneasy feeling, but didn't know why. She couldn't imagine why the police would be at the station.

Tameka saw her manager nod his head in her direction and police officers immediately started walking towards her. The two men in suits were walking with the cops. As they approached her, two of the officers drew their weapons. Tameka didn't know what to think. The two men in suits turned out to be detectives and they notified her of that as they got closer to her.

"Miss Williams, I'm Detective Marcus and we're going to need for you to come with us."

In a panic Tameka dropped her things and attempted to run for the stairs. But she was grabbed by the third officer.

"Tameka Williams, you are under arrest for the murder of Titus Grant."

Tameka continued to fight with the officers. She cried,

kicked and screamed and couldn't believe that her station manager had the camera's rolling. What a disgrace, instead of delivering the news, Tameka would be the headline story.

Tameka was cuffed and dragged out of the building only to find news crews from every other local station waiting to get a glimpse of her. She tried to hide her face, but everyone saw her anyway. Her makeup was running down her face in an ocean of tears. Her stockings were ripped and hanging from her legs. Tameka Williams was a mess and was being held in front of the cameras for the whole world to see. As she turned her head to try and look away, she spotted Brook, Eric and Mia in the crowd. They seemed to have been enjoying themselves immensely. The three looked as if they were at the movies watching a hysterical comedy.

Across town, Ms. Williams was watching the news as she cleaned the kitchen. When she saw her only daughter on television crying and in handcuffs she dropped the glass that she was holding. She was in absolute shock. Then when they stated the charges against Tameka, Ms. Williams fell to the floor in a puddle of tears. Her heart was broken.

Hours passed and Tameka was still in lock up without a clue as to how the police found out about Titus. They had interrogated her, but she refused to talk without an attorney present. She had called Wayne and he assured her that he would get an attorney to her as soon as possible. Finally, an officer came to get her. "Your attorney is here," was all the cop said as he cuffed her and escorted her back to an interrogation room.

"Miss Williams, I'm Attorney Frank Montz. I'm here to represent you."

"When can you get me out of here?" Tameka asked anxiously.

"It's not that simple, Miss Williams. They have you on tape killing a man. That's all the proof they need. You need to start thinking in terms of plea bargain."

"What tape? I don't understand any of this. Where did this tape come from?"

"Your landlord found it in the condo you were renting and turned it in. She's still in shock that she lived with and then rented to a murderer. She says she just wants justice to be served."

"That bitch, she set me up. Can't you see that?"

"What I see is a video tape with my client on it killing a man. Can you explain that?"

"It was self-defense; he was trying to rape me."

"On the tape it looks like he's trying to put you out when you stab him with broken glass. And you don't even stop with one, you turn around and stab him again in the neck. If you go ahead and plead guilty, I can probably get the charges knocked down to man slaughter."

"And how much time is that?"

"Anywhere from ten to twenty years, it will be up to the judge."

"I can't go to prison, I just can't."

"Miss Williams, stop crying and listen to me good. If you go before a jury you will get life!"

A month later, Tameka was escorted into a court room filled with spectators and news cameras. She saw her mother sitting with Wayne and on the opposite side sat Brook, Mia, Eric and David. Even Monica and Craig were standing in the back of the court room. They had all come to see her demise. Only her mom and Wayne gave a crap about her and the outcome of this case. The judge entered the room and Tameka, along with her attorney, entered a plea of guilty for the manslaughter charge that had been brought against her. The judge looked at her in disgust and delivered his sentence.

"Miss Williams, I've seen the tape and find you to be an evil woman that deserves to spend the rest of your natural life in prison. Unfortunately, I can't make that happen, but I can and I do sentence you to fifteen years in prison with the mandate that you must serve at least seven of those years. This should give you plenty of time to reevaluate your life. We can only hope that you'll come out better than you're going in."

As they were preparing to take Tameka out of the court room, she turned and started screaming to Brook. "You Bitch, how could you stab me in the back like this. All I ever did was try to be your friend. I hate you! I hope your stupid ass burns in hell, you ignorant cow! This isn't over, I will get you back, I will pay you back!" Tameka was still yelling and kicking as they dragged her away. Ms. Williams sobbed openly and Brook couldn't help but feel saddened herself. She hated to see Ms. Williams so hurt and hated to see Tameka chained like an animal. But she was obviously mentally ill and maybe she could get some help in prison. After all Tameka had done to Brook and so many others, she still felt as though she was the one wronged.

# EPILOGUE

It had been four years since Tameka was taken away in chains. Her first six months were more difficult than she could have ever imagined. It took her that long to realize that staying in constant conflict with the guards and other prisoners was only going to hurt her more in the long run. Besides, the month she spent in isolation almost drove her crazy. She had nothing but her own deranged thoughts to keep her company.

Tameka missed her old life and only had her mother and Wayne to come for the occasional visit. They were her only connection to the outside world and tried their best to keep her abreast of everything going on. She most enjoyed her visits from Wayne. She couldn't believe that he stayed with her through all of this. Even after he saw the tape playing on the news, he chose to give her the benefit of the doubt. She was confident in his love and felt secure in the fact that he'd be waiting for her when she got out. Her mother's visits tended to sometimes annoy her. Tameka did not take comfort or pleasure in the fact that Brook was still in contact with her mom. She didn't like that Brook was sending her mom monthly checks to help her out with the bills. She would rather see her mom struggle and be put out in the street than to have Brook caring for her. Brook had already taken everything from Tameka and now she was trying to take her mom.

Brook had actually contemplated going to see Tameka once. Not only did Eric protest, but so did Ms. Williams. Ms. Williams acknowledged to Brook that Tameka obviously had problems that she knew nothing about and could not fix. Ms. Williams practically begged Brook to just stay away from Tameka and move on with her life. She wanted to see Brook enjoying her loving husband, beautiful two year old daughter and precious six month old boy. They had a dream home that you only saw in pictures and those were the things that Brook needed to concern herself with. Ms. Williams felt blessed that Brook didn't hold Tameka's evil doings against her. She felt lucky that Brook cared enough to help her out and spend time with her so that she wasn't all alone in the world.

Mia had finally agreed to marry David. They were wed in an extravagant ceremony thrown by Brook and Eric a year after Tameka's conviction. The newlyweds had purchased a new home for themselves and were living comfortably. The most joyous part of their lives now was the anticipation of the birth of their first child.

Tameka was counting down her time. Maybe the next three years would fly by faster than she imagined they would. Maybe her new prison job in the warden's office would be enough to give her hope for the future. Maybe the counselor she had been assigned to would be able to help her see and understand her mistakes and correct her behavior and way of thinking. Maybe not.

# ACKNOWLEDGMENTS

I must first thank my God in Heaven above for all of the goodness and mercy that He has shown me throughout my life.

Thank you, Kenneth and Joshua Lee. I love you guys with my whole heart and your support means everything to me. Thank you, Mother (Myrtice Covington) for being you, for loving and sacrificing everything for your children. I must offer a big thank you to my dear friend, Cassandra Smith, for giving me the push I needed and for cheering me on every step of the way. Tim Covington, Carlos Covington, and Tiffany Foster, we are what's left, let the bond never be unbroken. I must offer my sincere thanks and gratitude to all of those that have offered their encouragement and support throughput this journey,

To the independent publishers and fellow writers that have shared wisdom, imparted knowledge, gave an encouraging word, sound advice, and even painful lessons, I thank you all.

## ALSO BY STACEY COVINGTON-LEE

The Knife In My Back 2

Bitter Taste Of Love

Hate The Way He Loves Me

When Love Ain't Enough

The Love That Lies Between Us

Coming summer 2019, her much anticipated novel, He Won't Go.

For bookings please email inquires@staceycovingtonlee.com.